WISDOM TO DEFEAT THE ENEMY

LAURA GAGNON

CONTENTS

ABOUT THE AUHOR

Laura Gagnon is a woman called by God to function as a kingdom ambassador, declaring the Word of the Lord. God uses her gift to write Holy Spirit-breathed prayers and apostolic decrees, teaching and equipping the body of Christ, and inner healing and deliverance ministry. Laura is blessed with the gift of understanding God's restorative work through her own personal experiences.

Once bound by bitterness, witchcraft, rejection, shame, and defeated mindsets, she now works with others to help them obtain their healing and deliverance. Laura is a witness to God's incredible love and knows firsthand the power of His grace. Through her insights and revelation, God has led Laura to influence many individuals into a restored relationship with Jesus Christ and has seen the power of God work miracles.

She is a woman that stands on the promises of God, encourages in others an elevated expectation of the miraculous and declares the gift of His life.

Laura is married and lives in Lake Elsinore, California with her family. She also writes for her blog Xpect a Miracle Ministries (formerly known as Beyond the Barriers) at: xpectamiracle.blogspot.com.

PREFACE

This book was designed to be used as a curriculum for a series of weekly inner healing and deliverance classes. I created this manual because people I taught on these subjects asked for the material to be put in a book. They wanted a resource they could refer back to for further study. Ideally, it should be taught by someone that understands deliverance issues and has prior experience in this area, and can be present to help answer any questions that may arise from class participants. However, I also recognize the need for this information to be available for those that don't have access to a class that covers this type of teaching. Many churches do not teach on deliverance, and there is a great void in the body of Christ for this sort of teaching.

Some people prefer to work through their issues with the Lord privately, and I believe that they can if they have the right teaching material available. What is contained here is how the Lord worked with me and the revelation that has come as a part of my own personal journey. What He has done in me, He can do in others, too. The Holy Spirit is our best source of help, and Jesus is a very patient teacher. May you receive the truth and revelation that makes you free, healed, and wiser than your enemy!

This book contains a great deal of information on a variety of topics, but there are still many aspects of a person's healing and deliverance that aren't continually stressed throughout the chapters. The power of praise, worship, and intimacy in our personal prayer life greatly impacts our ability to overcome spiritual oppression. Declarations of God's promises are also powerful and effective at releasing breakthroughs. Building an altar of personal worship in one's life is a key aspect of healing, because when God shows up with His presence, He always comes with healing. He always comes with revelation. He always shows up with the truth. It's the very nature of who He is, and He never shows up without releasing some aspect of His virtue. When we learn to steward the presence of God in our lives, breakthrough naturally follows. Each one of these things is a different, vital component in the life of the believer.

INTRODUCTION

Our Father knows that people want to live free from demonic oppression, and He has provided the wisdom needed so that we can outwit the enemy and live a victorious life in Christ. When a person makes a choice to live for Christ, then a new law takes effect, and under that new law, it is written in Romans 8:1: "Therefore, now no condemnation awaits those who are living in Jesus the Anointed, the Liberating King." The law of the Spirit of Life breathes into them and liberates that person from the law of sin and death.

The ability to live in our new nature is because we walk according to the movement of the Spirit in our lives. There are many people who understand this truth, yet they continue to live oppressed by the enemy. They still struggle with defeated mindsets and toxic emotions. Prayers seem to be blocked by invisible barriers they can't quite figure out. There seems to be a death grip on their finances, or they struggle with unexplained health issues. It could be a number of things that indicate the enemy somehow has found a way to hinder their prayers, but they can't quite figure out why. Questions such as, "What am I missing?" and "Why can I not seem to get the victory?" are often left unanswered, leaving people to come up with reasonable-sounding explanations as to why their prayers aren't answered. The problem with this is that without correct understanding, the answers people come up with are often from their own imagination and are drawn from unbelief or uncertainty instead of being based on truth.

God does not send answers to prayer if we are in agreement with unbelief. Unbelief stems from root issues in a person's life that causes their faith to be uncertain or unstable. God allows us to struggle with these things until we resolve the lies in our belief system. It takes faith to please God and receive answers to prayer! The scriptures remind us that if we have faith without doubt, then we can move mountains, but a double-minded man is unstable in all his ways and cannot expect to receive anything from the Lord. The correct response to difficult, stubborn situations is not to make up our own excuses as to why prayer is not answered, but to dig deeper into the scripture until we receive a clear answer from God, helping us become more successful in obtaining answered prayer. He promises us that if we ask for wisdom, He will grant it.

No one has to live feeling defeated. Christ came as an answer for our sin issues. He provided the answers to heal our bodies and restore our souls. He can enable us to live victoriously. Defeat, discouragement, and shame are not our portion! It's not our future. God has promised that He has a good plan for our lives, to give us a future and a hope. His word also promises that blessing awaits us when we are cleansed from the things that bring defilement.[1] The ruins of our lives will be rebuilt, and we will flourish. You may be one faith-filled declaration away from a breakthrough. Healing may be only one revelation away. Your very next prayer could be just the one that releases you from your chains and brings you through a new level of transformation, but unless you ask for wisdom and revelation, your victory in answered prayer may seem just out of reach. My prayer is that you become wiser than your adversary so that you continuously outwit him. May your faith carry you beyond every barrier and into the light of God's truth, and may you recover everything that belongs to you!

---

[1] Ezekiel 36:33-36

CHAPTER ONE
THE IDENTITY ISSUE

In order for a person to be able to help anyone else, they must first understand themselves. The most practical advice I can give anyone is that this is a subject that must begin with the individual. Yes, there are things that can be taught in a classroom; however, there is a big difference between being taught head knowledge and what is gained through actual experience. It is the experience that teaches us unforgettable life lessons. God wastes nothing. He will take every situation where the enemy got one over on us, robbed us, destroyed something precious, and used others in his plots to wound us. Our Father will teach us what He wants us to understand from those painful lessons, heal us, and then turn it right around to use as a weapon against the enemy, so that we can pull his house down and take back all the spoils of war!

In order for you, the reader, to be able to guide someone through inner healing and deliverance, then you must be willing to walk the path yourself. No other experiences have the ability to expose weaknesses in our character and our belief system than pain and adversity. Adversity is a good teacher. God allows difficult situations to shake our belief system because that is what exposes deeply rooted issues that destabilize our faith. The frustration that comes from a lack of answers challenges us to grow in our personal walk with Christ. Disappointment teaches us where our faith is anchored in the wrong things and uncovers lies that God is uprooting out of our lives. Rejection and betrayal teach us how to handle life situations with others, either with integrity and Christ-likeness, or reveals where we have a deficit in our ability to love others. In order to understand others, we must first understand our own weaknesses.

Without compassion for those who are suffering, a sense of pride and judgment will be reflected that can end up hurting others. God's desire is to use every little thing we might think is inconsequential to deliver us from pride, selfish ambition, critical judgments, and other things that would compromise the purity of our hearts and ministry to others. That is why there are some key foundational issues that each person must understand about themselves before they can attempt to guide someone else through their process. Deliverance ministry is not for the novice. It is for those that have experienced deliverance from bondage and have made a commitment to living a sanctified life. While anyone can pray for others, it is also important to have a proper sense of understanding about spiritual warfare issues. The single most important factor is understanding your identity in Christ.

The great thing about this teaching manual is that it can be used by anyone that is willing to learn and apply the wisdom from God's word. Whether you are using it for yourself or to teach and train others, it does take a commitment to research the scriptures that are provided so that you can understand the content and the context of what is written. It also requires each person to exercise their faith towards working through the prayers that are provided. The prayer of faith from a contrite heart is an acceptable sacrifice to God. The prayers help sever demonic attachments that can lead to oppression and blocked prayers, but they also restore a person to the right alignment with the heart of God, making room for God to move in the individual's life. Let's move forward on the topic of identity.

◆◆◆

There are no perfect parents. The majority of families have some level of brokenness and dysfunction, leading people to carry the weight of negative experiences and emotions. When brokenness is left unhealed, the cycle continues into the next generation because brokenness creates a false belief system. The false belief system is at odds with the truth of God's word and is intended to distort the image we have of ourselves, God and others. When a person's identity and self-worth are anchored in the pain of negative experiences, the enemy uses the pain of disappointment, injustice, and other negative emotions to rewrite a person's version of the truth.

Unhealed emotional wounds are the root issues behind rebellion, addictions, anger and abuse, generational poverty, violence, crime, and many other issues that reproduce brokenness. At the very heart of the issue is the orphan spirit, which leaves a gaping hole in the heart of the individual. The person is left yearning for a father's love, affirmation, and acceptance that will validate their sense of identity and self-worth.

Without a father's love and acceptance, the person often feels a sense of abandonment and may feel like they are wandering in life, never truly able to identify the root of their discontent and restlessness. They look for satisfaction and fulfillment in a variety of things, but nothing seems to fill the void. The person may tend to feel anxious, insecure, and unworthy. These 'feelings' often come from demonic spirits that lead people from place to place. Their assignment is to create distance, disillusionment, and disappointment between the individual, God, and others, perpetuating the cycle of brokenness.

The curse of the orphan spirit can be broken by a profound revelation of our heavenly Father's love and acceptance. Whether we can articulate it or not, our sense of longing for unconditional love and acceptance, and to be known and accepted for who we are, is the desire for intimacy. We long to be known and understood, and to be part of a healthy family. It originates in the heart of the Father, who longs for sons and daughters. God's heart is not just for **our** families to be healthy, but that we would be a part of **His** family. He, too, longs for us to truly **know Him** and understand His heart towards us. When we know His ways, we realize we can trust Him to provide leadership for our lives.

The family unit, with men fulfilling the father role and a woman fulfilling the role of the mother, is by divine design, because the male and female both impart different aspects of a child's identity, self-worth, and personal value. Fathers who are involved in their children's upbringing can add stability, confidence, and a sense of value to their children's lives. Children also take their cues from stimulating play and activity with their fathers, which sets a standard for how they regulate their emotions, attitudes, and interactions with others. Boys develop a sense of affirmation of the male role in family and society, and girls often receive an important aspect of their identity and esteem from healthy interactions with their fathers.

If a parent is absent, abusive, or neglectful towards their child, the child often internalizes rejection, abandonment, and insecurity, which affects their self-image and level of self-esteem. A child's social development is developed from the interactions with the male and female influences in their lives. When certain aspects of healthy role models are missing or distorted, there is confusion over what role the children play and how they are supposed to fit into society. Without strong male role models, children look to fill the void with the gender roles they are familiar with, whether or not they are healthy, nurturing, or affirming in their God-ordained identity.

The orphan spirit carries with it a feeling of abandonment and unworthiness, so the individual that is bound by this spirit often feels driven by the need to prove to themselves or others they have a sense of value and importance. They can easily get caught up in perfectionism and ambition because they are trying to compensate for feelings of inadequacy, inferiority, and insecurity. The struggle with the foundational issues of identity and the dysfunction it creates can cause relationship problems because the person may have an unhealthy or unrealistic perspective on how their emotional needs should be met. It can also result in placing unrealistic demands for validation and affirmation of their identity upon others, when in fact, only God can meet that need. When a person looks to other people instead of God to meet their emotional needs, they make idols for themselves. Idolatry always comes with consequences, because God is jealous for our affections. The individual can also display instability in their employment and career and be prone to addictions, eating disorders, or problems with authority.

The heart of the orphan has deeply rooted feelings of rejection and insecurity, which often causes them to have feelings of competitiveness and jealousy towards others. They compare themselves to others in their relationship circles, whether it is family, peer friendships, or professional relationships. They look for the praise and approval of others and often cannot bring themselves to genuinely celebrate other people's accomplishments. It is difficult for them to bless the successes of others because the spirit of competition is opposed to brotherly love. It sees people as rivals, and a fault-finding attitude is often present among competitors. The prodigal's elder brother saw his sibling as underserving because, in his estimation, he lived a more commendable life, while the younger lived a life of sin (ref. Luke 15:11-32).

The eldest brother's critical spirit and judgment of his brother's actions protested the validity of his father's judgment and eagerness to throw the lad a homecoming party. Although the blessings of sonship were always available to him, the spiritual deficit in the eldest son's life resulted in him seeing his brother through the lens of comparison and competition. The eldest, who exhibited the legalistic, religious attitude of qualifying for blessing based on his works, claimed his faithfulness in living a righteous life. He also exposed the weaknesses of his brother's sinful lifestyle. Both young men had the love of their father the entire time, yet they failed to realize the importance of being in the right relationship with him.

A religious spirit hinders people from connecting to the heart of the Father because the religious spirit emphasizes duty over relationship (see also ref. Luke 10:38-42). Those that compare their works to grace will stumble over their offenses. (ref. Rom. 9:31-33) The religious spirit always creates spiritual orphans because love, acceptance, and blessings all depend upon performance, not unconditional love.

Emotional and spiritual deficits can lead the individual to expose the weaknesses of others or accuse others so that they attempt to feel better about themselves. The person who struggles with an orphan spirit seeks to impress others in order to gain praise and recognition, because they desperately need to feel validated and affirmed. This sort of validation can only come from God because He is the One that created us. Only He has a pure and holy love. God's love does not come with mixed motives, so only our Father should be allowed to affirm us in our true identity as His son or daughter.

Rejection causes fear, instability, depression, anger, or episodes of rage. The heart of the person suffering from an orphan spirit often goes through life feeling a great deal of emotional pain that they find difficult to heal. This is because it is impossible to counsel a demonic spirit; it must be driven out through teaching & truth, breaking agreement with it, and driving out the evil spirit with prayer.

All of these things can result in a form of spiritual slavery. It is a mind-blinding spirit that works almost like a demonic magic spell, making people unaware that a form of deception is operating against them. If a person doesn't understand how to identify the real problem in their life, they don't know how to address it.

WISDOM TO DEFEAT THE ENEMY

This is how the enemy keeps people stuck in old cycles of defeat. There is a misconception that 'time heals everything,' but that is not true. Most of the time, the pain is just buried.

As time goes on, problems tend to worsen. The person ends up feeling like a victim rather than victorious. The person is chained in a spiritual prison they cannot get out of until the Spirit of Truth leads the person, by revelation, into the truth that finally sets them free. The following chart shows the differences between the heart of the orphan vs. the heart of the individual living as a son or daughter of God. Use it as a diagnostic tool to better understand yourself.

On a piece of paper, write down the things that you recognize in yourself that you know to be true. This is between you and God. Be honest in your assessment, then pray over what you have written down. Ask the Lord to show you anything that He sees in you that you might not have written down. Above all, please understand that the Lord is FOR YOU. It is not His will, nor mine, that you would be brought under condemnation, rather that your eyes would be opened so that you can receive the truth that will free you. For the convenience of those wanting to xerox this chart or use it as a handout, it has been moved to the next page.

Orphan Spirit	Spirit of Sonship
• Feels inadequate. Needs approval and strives for praise and acceptance from others.	• Receives approval through a relationship with God, and gives affirmation to others.
• Jealous and competitive, has a difficult time being happy for other people's successes and blessings.	• Celebrates other people's successes and accomplishments. Is genuinely happy when others are blessed.
• Insecure in who they are as a person, has trouble with a sense of personal worth due to a spirit of unworthiness and rejection.	• Secure with their identity because they walk in the revelation of God's unconditional love and acceptance.
• Critical and judgmental towards others and quick to expose the weaknesses of others. Inwardly they feel they need to do this in order to make themselves look better.	• Walks in love and grace towards others. Covers others in love.

• Has trouble trusting authority; has a lack of submission.	• Honors others and is respectful of authority.
• Closes their spirit to correction and discipline; defensive and easily offended.	• Recognizes the value of accountability in relationships and allows others to speak into their life.
• Keeps emotional walls up and remains guarded; never lets people get to know them.	• Open, trusting, looks for the good in others, and allows themselves to be vulnerable in relationships.
• Feels like they are under bondage to performance in order to receive approval. Often feels as if God is difficult to please. Feels like a slave, bound by a sense of duty and obligation.	• Walks in freedom from religious attitudes and constrictions. Feels like a son or daughter, and seeks to please God through their relationship, not performance or duty. Is a passionate lover of God.
• Seeks relief from external, counterfeit sources such as alcohol and drugs, shopping, sex, and other escapes. Seeks to escape negative emotions and feelings with false forms of comfort.	• Seeks comfort from the presence of God; allows Holy Spirit to minister to them. Looks for comfort in a relationship with the Father, Jesus, and Holy Spirit.
• Feels like they have to fight for what they want and will sometimes go to any length to get what they desire. Prone to using guilt, manipulation, condemnation, toxic shame or other negative tactics to try to force others into compliance. Driven by selfish ambition and a need for recognition and approval.	• Led by the Holy Spirit. Does not feel the need to strive for recognition, position, or promotions. Humble. Does not try to manipulate others for selfish gain. Trusts God to bless them in His due time; walks in the understanding of sonship and inheritance.

- Feels like they can never measure up, and it's difficult to please God. Struggles with rebellion towards God because of the belief that they aren't good enough to please Him.
- Feels a sense of abandonment and isolation, invisibility and unimportance.

- The orphan spirit speaks their spiritual poverty into the atmosphere. Statements such as "I'm an idiot," or "I'm stupid," or "You have never loved me," and "You care about _____ more than you care about me" are examples of unworthiness, competitiveness, and self-pity in the mind and heart of the orphan. Statements are laced with accusations in order to manipulate the emotions of others. Individual covers their sense of inadequacy with pride and an overinflated sense of self-importance (for show).

- An orphan spirit will repel spiritual or natural children. This comes from the deep-rooted fear of trying to overcome a sense of rejection, disapproval, or anger when a person's inner needs are not met. The unhealthy demand for emotional

- Secure in their identity in Christ, submitted heart attitude towards God.

- Is connected to others in healthy, life-giving relationships. Is free from ambition and the need to seek validation from external sources. Understands that their Father 'sees' them and that they are not invisible.

- The affirmation of being adopted into the family of God causes the son or daughter to feel confident that they have value in the eyes of God and others. Their self-esteem is not at risk, nor is their personal worth based on emotions or what others think about them, but rather their position as God's child.

- The Spirit of sonship is based on love, peace, and acceptance and attracts others because the love of the Father is evident. Sons & Daughters do not look to others to fulfill their needs for validation but

validation becomes toxic to the relationship.	receive it from their Father. Speaks words of faith and confidence is
• Leaders who operate under an orphan spirit seek to have others serve them; they do not release people into their destiny. They hold onto them due to a need to build their own kingdom. They need to feel needed.	• Spiritual fathers and mothers that operate with a right understanding of their heavenly father seek to release others into their calling and destiny. They genuinely want the best interests of others and do not feel threatened by the success of others.
• Compares their works of righteousness to righteousness through faith. Their offenses become a stumbling block.	• The cornerstone of their faith is anchored in what Christ has done on the Cross.

Now that you have reviewed the characteristics of an orphan spirit vs. the spirit of sonship, it's important to address those things in prayer. Simply being aware of those things is not enough. Ask God to forgive you for wrong beliefs, elevating what others have said about you, or negative assessments of yourself that you have agreed with rather than the truth of His word.

THE ORPHAN SPIRIT, OFFENSE, AND SPIRITUAL AGREEMENTS

As previously discussed, one of the characteristics of the orphan spirit is a tendency towards holding onto offense and critical judgments towards oneself and others. Sometimes it comes from being treated unjustly, as in cases of neglect or some form of abuse. It can also come from various other causes; however, the orphan spirit is a root cause for people feeling jealous, critical, or bitter. They simply don't understand why life seems so hard, or why it feels like they have to wrestle for every bit of progress and fight for every little bit of blessing. It hurts to feel like you have to fight for everything, and it causes jealousy towards others that seem like they get blessed without even trying. The misunderstanding of who and what people are wrestling against can make them angry, disappointed, and bitter, especially if that person feels like they are doing everything they know how to do to live with integrity. Those feelings cause offense, and sometimes the offended feelings are directed towards God. We blame Him for our lack of understanding, and the fact that we feel worn out from trying to survive when we long to **prosper and thrive**.

The problem is not that God doesn't understand our pain; it's the fact that our pain sometimes causes us to accuse God of being unfair. The culmination of those feelings can cause us to lose hope and feel like we will never break free from the limitations set against us. That is when the offense can really set in, whether it's towards God or someone else, but when we retain offense, it makes us vulnerable to allowing our mouths to be used for the enemy's purposes. Offended people will come into agreement with the spirit of accusation, and that puts them in alignment with 'the accuser,' also known as Satan. God cannot bless what is in agreement with Satan.

Gossip and slander come from the word 'diabolos,' or the Strong's Greek #1228, **diaballo**; meaning to slander, accuse, or defame someone unjustly, criticizing to hurt or condemn in order to sever a relationship. Devil or 'diabollo' refers to 'one who divides.' A person that is overtaken with gossip and talebearing has partnered with Satan for the purpose of tearing down someone else's reputation. The intent to destroy may or may not be intentional, but the enemy's intended result is destruction in one form or another. Gossip, slander, backbiting, whispering, and talebearing are sins of assassinating the character, reputation, and livelihood of another person. This is why Jesus equated it with murder and cautioned his disciples to be careful that they did not come under judgment from careless use of their words.

Matt. 12:36   "But I tell you that every idle word man shall speak, they shall give an account in the day of judgment."

Prov. 10:18   "He who conceals hatred has lying lips, and he who spreads slander is a fool."

Ps. 101:5   "Whoever secretly slanders his neighbor, him I will destroy. No one who has a haughty look or an arrogant heart will I endure."

Prov. 18:8   "The words of a whisperer (gossip) are like dainty morsels (to be greedily eaten. They go down into the innermost chambers of the body (to be remembered and mused upon)."

1 John 2:11   "But he who hates his brother is in darkness and walks in darkness, and does not know where he is going, because the darkness has blinded his eyes."

Eph. 4:31   "Let all bitterness and wrath and anger and clamor and slander be put away from you, along with all malice."

Prov. 16:28   "A perverse man sows strife; and a whisperer separates chief friends."

Matthew 7:1 tells us that we should not judge lest we also come under the same judgment. When people use their mouths to curse or defame others, to slander or gossip, it is usually because they find something offensive in another person, and then they expose whatever weaknesses are in that individual. According to the principle of Matthew 7:1, the person that is holding on to a negative judgment against someone else is now on a path to be judged, either by God or others. When a person's weaknesses are exposed, it allows others to see the insincerity between what they have judged in someone else and the hypocrisy of their own actions. Many times, what happens is that the thing we are tempted to judge in someone else eventually comes back to haunt us. I can't tell you how many times I have judged someone else's actions and then sometime later had the sudden realization that I was guilty of doing the same exact thing.

It really is a good reminder that none of us are perfect, and none of us are qualified to sit as a judge over someone else. As humbling as it is at times, I thank God for His grace and love that shows me when I am wrong, because then I can repent and confess my sin. Confession clears the record of wrongs that the enemy may try to use as legal grounds to withstand our prayers. Angels are not the only ones that record our conversations and actions. The enemy scrutinizes us, watches, and waits for an inroad into our lives. Demons are scribes that record our sins and weaknesses so as to use things against us at a later date. The things we do that violate scripture become the legal grounds the enemy needs to enforce a curse. All curses ARE broken through the cross of Jesus Christ; however, it is our obedience that insures God's hedge of protection around us. If we break the principles of scripture, we become vulnerable to receiving the fruit of our deeds, and sometimes that means we have opened ourselves up to the enforcement of a curse, not by God, but by the enemy.

There are occasions when the tongue needs deliverance. In Acts chapter 2, the Holy Spirit descended upon believers, and immediately what was affected was the tongue. They were baptized by the Holy Spirit with 'tongues of fire,' which filled the believers with power so that they became effective witnesses to the world. Satan also tries to counterfeit a spiritual reality, but in a different way. James 3:6 tells us, "The tongue also is a fire, a world of wickedness among the parts of the body. It pollutes the whole person and sets the course of his life on fire, and is itself set on fire by hell."

`Prov. 18:21   "Life and death are in the power of the tongue, and those that love it will eat its fruit."

Prov. 21:23   "He who guards his mouth and tongue keeps his soul from distress."

When our conversation isn't sanctified, it diminishes the power of our witness, and it also pollutes our whole person. As we can see from scripture, there are definite consequences for allowing our words to be unwholesome. Many times, people don't even realize that the power of their words and thoughts keep them from being healed because there is an agreement with the demonic realm that must first be broken. Sometimes those agreements go all the way back to our childhood or some traumatic event.

Many people try to bury their feelings, and they no longer realize that the pain from the trauma is still alive. It's hidden, but it's still there, and pain always looks for a way to manifest. Sometimes it affects our physical bodies, too, because the body often absorbs the pain. A great deal of physical illness and disease are rooted in spiritual issues. Physical and emotional pain is an indicator that something is wrong. There is a wound that needs healing. Pain does not just go away on its own; it must be driven out through the power of prayer. This is what releases the healing.

Taming the tongue requires repentance, confession, and submitting our tongue to the authority of the Holy Spirit. We must remove the legal grounds that allow the enemy to enforce some form of punishment. Let me give you an example. I was ministering to a woman that still felt regret and grief over marrying a man that molested her children. Although her children were now grown and had families of their own, she felt responsible for their brokenness because she had unknowingly married a pedophile when her children were very young. Many years later, she was still carrying the guilt and suffering from the repressed feelings of anger, bitterness, and abuse they had all suffered during a very traumatic period in their lives. She had trouble forgiving herself for the pain that had been caused to her children, and she made the comment, "I deserve this punishment."

Demonic spirits had taken her words and formed their assignment. Her body was being tormented and inflicted with various sicknesses and infirmities, but there was also a great deal of emotional torment. Finally, after many prayers, she was able to resist the enemy and renounce the ungodly agreements she had made. She forgave herself and her offender. She repented for believing the lies that she needed to be punished because Jesus took our punishment upon Himself when He went to the cross. Those spirits did not want to let her speak, but Jesus helped win the victory. She felt immensely different after breaking those agreements, which allowed her to take authority over the enemy and command all those tormenting devils to leave her! It was very difficult for her to try to take authority over the evil spirits because she never felt confident in exercising the dominion God gave her. Passivity strengthened the enemy's grip on her. Notice that the demons didn't directly attack her identity; they used a painful situation that caused her to grieve with regret for many years, but it was her identity that was still under assault. When a person believes lies about themselves or feels inferior, they will not resist the enemy. Instead, they will form some sort of agreement with demonic spirits. That is how the enemy continues to manipulate the person from an orphan mindset. (Examples: "I'm weak," "I am not good enough…look what I did," "I am stupid for allowing this to happen.")

BREAKING UNGODLY AGREEMENTS

It is important to repent for any agreements that have been made knowingly or unknowingly with the enemy, because those agreements have given demonic spirits legal grounds to carry out their assignments. Repent, renounce and declare that you break the agreement with him. Tell Satan you divorce him and all his evil cohorts, and you will no longer serve them. Let them know they are not your master, spouse, or friend, and they cannot stay. Jesus instructed us to 'bind the strongman' before we could plunder his house and recover the spoils of war (ref. Mark 3:27). Jesus was clearly illustrating the fact that the enemy seeks to inhabit a 'house' and people represent that house.

Many of the spirits listed on the next page are strongman spirits. They are like Satan's generals, and they all have a host of other demons working under their authority. Bind them and cast them out, commanding all underling spirits to 'be bound in Jesus's name' and command them to leave as well. You must tell them to leave in the name and authority of Jesus Christ and let them know they are forbidden from coming back. You will find a prayer at the end of the chapter.

_ The Spirit of Fear

_ The Orphan Spirit

_ Spirit of Rejection

_ Spirit of Broken Heart

_ Spirits of Loneliness and Isolation

_ Spirits of Jealousy, Rivalry, and Competition

_ Spirits of Unbelief, Double-Mindedness, Poverty, and Death

_ Spirits of Selfish Ambition, Comparison, and Envy

_ Spirit of Haughtiness and Pride

_ Spirits of Dishonor, Disapproval, and Disappointment

_ Spirits of Anger and Rage

_ Spirits of Bondage, Alcohol, Pharmacia, and Addiction

_ Spirits of Accusation, Criticism, and Judgment

_ Spirit of Unforgiveness and Bitterness

_ Spirits of Rebellion and Idolatry

_ Spirit of Confusion

_ Mind-Blinding and Octopus Spirits

_ Spirits of Self-Pity and Victim Spirit

_ Spirits of Shame, Guilt, and Condemnation

_ Spirits of Past and Regret

_ Spirit of Python

_ Spirit of Heaviness

_ Spirits of Unloving and Unwanted

_ Spirits of Whoredom, Idolatry, and Witchcraft

_ All lying and familiar spirits

God designed human beings to gain their sense of identity and their sense of security from their heavenly Father. We receive this as a revelation when we walk in relationship with Him. It is a truth that is received deep in our innermost being where our Spirit bears witness with the Holy Spirit. This knowledge brings comfort, and as we are comforted, our souls settle down into rest. When our souls are at rest, the result is stability.

Every Christian will experience the contradiction between what scripture says is ours by faith and the adjustment period of learning to live in that reality. 2 Corinthians 5:17 tells us that if anyone is in Christ, they are a new creation. Transformation is a process that requires our cooperation. The conflict between who we used to be and who we are in the process of becoming lies in our understanding. We don't attempt to keep the old version of ourselves alive because our old identity is directly associated with sin and shame. We don't try to keep making a better version of who we used to be; we must let our former selves die so that we can walk in a brand-new identity.

Jesus set us free – He won the victory for us on the cross, but we must take decisive action in order to lay claim to the finished work of Christ. We must learn to think and act differently, but we cannot do that if we still operate out of an old belief system. That is why it is vital to our understanding to know our true identity.

As Jesus died our death on the cross, the blood of a holy God was shed for all mankind. When He was resurrected, we were resurrected with Him. That is why the scripture says, "I have been crucified with Christ. It is no longer I who live, but Christ lives in me.; and the life that I now live in the flesh I live by faith in the Son of God, who loved me and gave His life for me." Galatians 2:20

WHAT HAS THE BLOOD OF JESUS DONE FOR US?

The blood of Jesus has **paid our debt** once and for all. Heb. 9:28

The blood of Jesus **redeems** us through forgiveness of sins. Eph. 1:7

Taking **communion** and partaking of Jesus's blood **makes us spiritually alive**. John 6:53.

The blood of Jesus **heals** us. 1 Peter 2:24

The blood of Jesus **purifies** us from all sin. 1 John 1:7

The blood of Jesus **gives us hope, citizenship and brings us near to God**. Eph. 2:12-13.

The blood of Jesus **exchanges my sin for His righteousness**. 2 Cor. 5:21.

The blood of Jesus **cleanses my consciousness from guilt**. Heb. 10:22.

The blood of Jesus gives me **victory.** Rev. 12:11.

Jesus took all of mankind's suspicion, distrust, hostility, and pride, and through His blood, destroyed the wall of separation to bring reconciliation. Through offering His body upon the cross, Jesus demonstrated His willingness to let love kill all the hostility and build a bridge back to our heavenly Father. This act of humility and love allowed us to become family. Not only have we become family, but we are adopted as sons and daughters of God and heirs to a kingdom. Our new identity is one of royalty.

The word of God was given to us to separate our flesh from our spirit so that we could become more like Christ. "For the word of God is alive and active. Sharper than any double-edged sword, it penetrates even to dividing soul and spirit, joints and marrow; it judges the thoughts and attitudes of the heart." Heb. 4:12 NIV.

Let's do a little practice exercise to help uncover some lies that may be in your belief system. You will want to write down your answers and perhaps do some journaling to help you process your feelings and responses.

Close your eyes and envision yourself walking around heaven. This is your homeland. Imagine the colors, the sound of worship, and the incredible love of God that is evident in everything around you. The flowers, trees, and plants are vibrant in color and alive. You hear them singing and praising Jesus! Your heart leaps with joy, and it's the most pleasurable feeling you've ever experienced. Your Father's love is so strong, it's tangible. You can feel it penetrating every part of you, wrapping itself around you like a warm, comforting blanket. The flowers, the gardens, and the beauty of heaven is like nothing you've ever experienced before! See yourself walking in the garden, running your fingers through the cool, refreshing fountain and smelling the fragrance of the lovely flowers.

An angel shows you the enormous buildings of treasures and undelivered gifts that God has for His people, but many never receive because of their unbelief. The angel shows you warehouses of extra body parts with names on them, ready to be given to their rightful recipients should they need them. As you explore heaven, you have a sense of amazement that your Father's plans for your future are impeccable. Every detail is accounted for and is set aside, marked with individual names of who it belongs to. You pass by an entire building with your name on the door, and you are struck with wonder.

The angel gives you a knowing glance, communicating that everything in that building is set aside for you! You see an intricate and beautiful castle with the most amazing architecture, like nothing you have seen before. It is truly out of this world! Gold, silver, exquisite jewels, and pearls all make up the astounding beauty of the building, and it's absolutely breathtaking. Although you've never been in this castle, it feels like home. As you approach the huge, majestic doors, they open wide, almost as if they instinctively sense you walking towards them. A variety of angels come and go about their important duties. One greets you with a message that your Father, the King, would like to see you. *Pause*. Please be ready to write down your answers to the following questions.

QUESTIONS FOR CONSIDERATION AND DISCUSSION

1. What thoughts come to mind? How do you see yourself now, after exploring a different reality in heaven? Does imagining a different reality inspire your faith to believe for more and take God at His word?

2. How do you feel knowing that Jesus has prepared a place for you to come home to?

3. Do you find yourself struggling to believe that the castle was your home? How does this image of royalty conflict with the way you were raised or the way you tend to see yourself?

4. What feelings or emotions do you need to resolve before you can see yourself in a new light, with a new identity?

5. List any emotions you may feel that are tied to your old identity. Ex: unworthy, rejection, abandonment, neglected or orphan, unlovable, unwanted.

Let's shatter the lies with the truth of God's word. This is just a partial list of some of the thoughts or feelings you may experience. If you write something down that isn't listed here, you will want to find an appropriate scripture that refutes the lie of the enemy.

Unworthiness – What does scripture say about this? Let's not forget that even Jesus's disciples had some moments when they felt unworthy, too. Peter denied Christ at a moment when his faith was tested, but Jesus forgave him and restored him. Peter definitely felt convicted and unworthy, but Jesus helped him get past his failures. The Apostle Paul also felt unworthy when he said, "For I am the least of the apostles, who am not worthy to be called an apostle, because I persecuted the church of God. But by the grace of God I am what I am, and His grace towards me was not in vain, but I labored more abundantly than them all, yet not I, but the grace of God which was with me." 1 Cor. 15:9-10.

When people feel unworthy, it's because they are broken inside, so what does God say about the brokenhearted? "For He heals the brokenhearted and binds up their wounds." Ps. 147:3

Feelings of not being 'good enough' or unworthy can be connected to feelings of guilt, shame, or regret for things we have done, and the guilt and condemnation need to be cleansed from our conscience. It is also important to understand that sometimes people unknowingly make a covenant with the spirit of regret, which can keep them stuck in the past. Shame, guilt, and condemnation make it difficult for the person to forgive themselves for past mistakes. This, too, is part of the poverty mindset that works alongside the orphan spirit.

The poverty mindset makes it difficult to move past mistakes and tends to grieve over them long after a sufficient time has passed, and the person should be able to move on.

The enemy loves to use shame and regret to keep people stuck in the past. We must be careful not to form agreements with those spirits! We need to understand that the Holy Spirit in our lives does not continue to inflict punishment on our conscience; only the enemy does that. When the conscience is cleansed through confession and repentance, the soul is then free to return to peace and joy. Peace and joy are a by-product of repentance, because it is our conscience that testifies whether or not we are in the right relationship with God. 1 John 3:32 says, "Beloved, if our hearts do not condemn us, we have confidence towards God," and "If we confess our sins, He is faithful and just to forgive us of sin and cleanse us of all unrighteousness" 1 John 1:9.

If you feel small and insignificant, remember how God takes care of the little sparrows. They do not feel frantic with worry or fear over whether or not they will have what they need. God provides all that they need. "Fear not, therefore, for you are of more value than the sparrow" Matt. 10:31.

When Jesus traded His life for ours, His sacrificial death imputed value to us. If it did not, then He would have died in vain. The Lord gave His life because of His LOVE for us. "For God so loved the world that He gave His only begotten Son, that whosoever believes in Him would not perish but have everlasting life" John 3:16.

Rejection – The people in our lives may not meet our need for love and acceptance, but every need can be fulfilled in Christ. The truth, according to Ephesians 1:6, is that you are accepted in the beloved. So, you were bought with a price, and you are dearly loved by God!

"For the Lord will not reject His people; He will never forsake His inheritance" Ps. 94:14.

God has loved us and known us from the very beginning, even if we were not aware of His hand upon us. "For You created my inmost being; You knit me together in my mother's womb. I praise You because I am fearfully and wonderfully made. Your works are wonderful, that I know full well" Ps. 139:13-14.

The Bible tells us that we may be rejected by some people, but we are chosen by God and precious to Him, according to 1 Peter 2:4. If the Creator of the Universes has chosen us, then who is man to reject us? Although we may experience the pain of rejection from others, the very fact that GOD himself has chosen us to love and accept into His family is a much more powerful truth.

Jesus said, "All that the Father gives Me will come to Me, and the one who comes to Me I will by no means cast out" John 6:37.

Abandonment, Neglected/Orphan – No matter what we may face in life, our Father wants us to be strong and courageous, knowing that He is with us. "Be strong and of good courage; do not fear nor be afraid of them for the Lord your God, He is the one that goes with you. He will not leave you nor forsake you" Deut. 31:6.

We are God's children, and His heart and affections are towards us. Even if our own parents fail to meet our emotional needs, God has said, "Can a woman forget her suckling child, that she should not have compassion on the son of her womb? Surely, they may forget you, yet I will not forget you. See, I have inscribed you on the palm of my hands; your walls are continually before Me" Is. 49:15-16.

"Though my mother and father abandoned me, the Lord gathers me up" Ps. 27:10.

 "Let your conduct be without covetousness; be content with such things as you have, for He Himself has said, "I will never leave you or forsake you. So, we may boldly say, The Lord is my helper. I will not fear. What can man do to me?" Heb. 13:5-6.

We have been adopted by our heavenly Father into the family of God. "All who are led by the Spirit of God are sons of God. For you did not receive the spirit of slavery to fall back into fear, but you have received the Spirit of Adoption as sons by whom we cry, 'Abba, Father!'" Romans 8:14-15.

Unlovable/Unwanted – "See what love the Father has lavished upon us, that we should be called children of God! And that is what we are! The reason the world does not know us is that it did not know Him" 1 John 3:1.

"The Lord appeared to us in the past saying, "I have loved you with an everlasting love; I have drawn you with unfailing kindness" Jer. 31:3.

"Dear friends, let us love one another, for love is from God. Everyone that loves has been born of God and knows God" 1 John 4:7

Our true identity can only be understood as we have a relationship with God. If we don't have a very deep relationship with the Lord, then it becomes difficult to understand Him and to relate to Him. It also becomes difficult to understand how we are to walk in our new identity.

Our identity and how we perceive ourselves is not based on our achievements or mistakes, or our accomplishments or failures. It's not based on how other people see us, comments that others make towards us, or our own inward thoughts and feelings about ourselves. Our identity is not tied to what we do for a living, our social status, where we came from, or how we were raised. None of those things actually have any bearing on our true identity. Our identity is positional, based on how we are related to God, our Father.

IDENTIFYING THE POVERTY MINDSET

The poverty mindset comes from the spirits of poverty, death, and hell. It is a **fear-based belief system** that partners with unbelief, doubt, and anxiety. A poverty mindset works in partnership with the orphan spirit, causing the individual to place their agreement with the enemy without them realizing it. Sometimes this poverty mindset becomes so strong in an area that it is elevated in power, becoming a principality over an entire region.

This becomes quite evident in geographic areas that are prone to low-income levels, broken families, crime, and a sense of hopelessness over the future. A spirit of broken-heartedness overcomes the spirit of faith and causes people to accept their circumstances as their reality. A poverty spirit and the spirit of python are not always mentioned in the same conversation, but they do operate together. These factors cause the spirit of python, which is constriction, to literally squeeze the vitality and ability to prosper out of people.

The python spirit is a lying spirit of witchcraft. Like the serpent in the garden, it whispers lies to its victims, leading them into temptation to question what God has said in His word. It is a counterfeit voice of God known as divination (ref. Acts 16:16-18). Divination refers to 'divine,' or the implication that the source of inspired information is from a deity. That is why it can seem effective in counterfeiting the voice of God.

It can truly sound believable. It is also the source of clairvoyance, false prophecy, and ventriloquism. This spirit can even speak some aspects of truth, as in false prophecy, but because it comes from an **unholy origin,** it carries defilement and will defile those that receive those words as truth. In many cases, especially with those who have witchcraft in their family history, familiar spirits have been a part of people's lives since they can remember, making it difficult to identify. Some people mistake this as a gift from God because this voice does feed them information. Clairvoyants, mediums, and others may even insist they use it for good purposes, but ALL DEMONS ARE LIARS (ref. 1 John 4:1; 1 John 4:3; 1 Tim. 4:1; John 8:44; 2 Chron. 18:22).

When it comes to the spirit of python, the nature of the serpent is to constrict and crush its victim. The serpent coils around its victim. Every time the victim tries to inhale and catch its breath, the constrictor tightens its grip, literally crushing the ribs and making it impossible to breathe. When python wants to constrict someone's finances, this is often what it feels like. You feel like you're suffocating under the weight of financial constriction. Python is a principality that works to constrict people's faith, cause extreme tiredness and a sense of heaviness, constrict finances, and will wear people out.

The grip of the constrictor spirit causes people to feel fear and anxiety as if they can barely survive. The voice of the enemy convinces people to 'buy the lie' and believe they will never have enough, and they cannot afford to be generous in giving. This is how it works with a poverty mindset, too. The person that believes these lies will restrict their giving or not give at all, thereby cutting off their ability to reap the blessings of God.

The sowing and reaping principle is always in effect, so when we don't give, we can't receive. It further tightens the noose around our finances until we literally feel like we are being squeezed to death. The only way to break this death-grip is to intentionally resist the enemy and sow generously into the place that God directs you to give. Ask God where you should sow in order to get a kingdom reward!

The python spirit is attracted to our humanity or our old nature. Serpents flick out their tongue to sense their prey, and they also lick the dust (ref. Gen. 3:14). Dust speaks of humanity, because God formed mankind out of the dust of the earth (ref. Gen.2:7). The enemy always looks for ways to ensnare us or bring us into bondage, so the more of our old nature we display, (such as anger, complaining, or falling back into worldly behaviors) the more power we give away to demonic spirits, allowing them to gain a foothold in our lives. Python operates in pride, stubbornness, heaviness, depression, and bitterness (ref. Acts 8:23).

Python also works to steal worship away from God, and will wear people out so that they are so tired they just have no interest in prayer, worship, or getting into God's presence. This is one way it works against people to withstand their breakthroughs. The nature of a constrictor is to wear out its victim until its strength is gone. It can feel as though an invisible force is slowly squeezing the life force out of them. Some people also experience difficulty in breathing, back problems, heart attacks, and other physical manifestations.

The key to breakthrough is to intentionally do exactly what the enemy has been trying to prevent! Sow generously and consistently in the place the Lord directs you to give. Do not be manipulated by guilt or legalism but be divinely directed by the Spirit of God, because He knows where the fertile ground will produce a great harvest. Be intentional and pray, worship, and sing your praises to God, whether or not you feel like it. Defy the enemy!

Let's take a look at the characteristics of a poverty mindset as well as a soul that is prospering. You can use the following chart as a diagnostic tool. Write down any trademarks of a poverty mindset and belief system so that you can come back to it later and address those things in prayer.

Poverty Spirit	Healthy Soul/Faith-Filled Believer
• I will never have enough. I can't afford to be generous; I can't afford to give. Cuts off their own ability to reap because they don't sow.	• Trusts God to provide. Believes God's word, and practices a lifestyle of sowing and giving.
• Overwhelmed with anxiety and stress over circumstances.	• Has confidence towards God and 'casts their cares on God' because He cares for them.
• Believes circumstances are truth. Negative situations have rewritten their ideology.	• Believes God's word is truth and circumstances must bow to the higher authority of His word.
• Resigns themselves to accepting circumstances as their reality. Surrenders to hopelessness.	• Takes God's word and battles with it over their circumstances. Warrior spirit.
• Feels like they are constantly striving in life; feels like they have to resort to crime, theft, or other dishonorable behaviors in order to get what they want/feel they need.	• They know how to rely on Jesus and pray into their need, trusting God to provide for them.

- Hoarding behaviors, miserly, feels like they can't afford to let go of anything because they might need it someday.

- You are responsible for your own provision.

- Serves money. Mammon has become their god. Self-will and mammon are idols because they cannot fully trust God.

- Prone to impatience and impulse decisions due to a need for instant gratification.

- Never satisfied, always chasing influence, power, position, or material goods because identity and self-worth are tied to material possessions.

- Feels like a victim. Has poor self-image and understanding of personal value. Makes self-deprecating comments.

- Blesses others with what they have and is not controlled by anxiety over future needs.

- God is their source of all provision. Knows God as Jehovah Jireh (provider)

- Money serves them.

- Practices self-control over spending money and has a mature attitude towards money.

- Content with what they have. Identity is not connected to material positions, a sense of power, or competitiveness to be like others. Identity comes from knowing their position is secure as a child of God.

- Victorious in Christ. Has a healthy self-image and esteem without being filled with pride or arrogance. Confident in who they are in Christ.

Our identity can only be realized 'through Christ.' Our Creator made us in His image, according to Genesis 1:27. When we receive Jesus as our Lord and Savior, we are brought into the family of God. Our position is secure as a child of God because we are adopted. All the rights of inheritance are imputed to us. Whose image, then, should we reflect? Doesn't it make sense that the person that created us is the only One qualified to tell us who we are?

Ephesians 1:5 tells us that we are predestined to _____

1 Corinthians 12:27 tells us that we are each a part of _____

1 John 3:3 tells me I am _____

John 15:14 tells me I am _____

Colossians 1:14 tells me I am _____

Romans 8:17 tells me _____.

2 Cor, 1:21 tells me _____

Ephesians 2:6 tells me _____

2 Peter 1:4 tells me _____

Jesus gave us His delegated authority. "Behold I give authority to trample on serpents and scorpions, and over all the power of the enemy, and nothing shall hurt you" Luke 10:19.

"Truly I say to you, whatever you bind on earth shall be bound in heaven, and whatever you loose on earth shall be loosed in heaven. Again, I say to you, if two of you agree on earth about anything they ask, it will be done for them by my Father in heaven. For where two or more are gathered in My name, there I am among them" Matt. 18:18-20.

"And these signs will accompany those who believe: In My name they will cast out demons, they will speak in new tongues, they will pick up serpents in their hands; and if they drink any deadly poison, it will not hurt them, they will lay hands on the sick and they will recover" Mark 16:17-18.

When we pray, we don't have to beg God to do something. He has put His Spirit in us and has given us authority to declare His will 'on earth as it is in heaven.' We can be bold in prayer, knowing that we are 'in Christ' and that our Father expects us to reflect His image and nature as we go about doing the family business! The Greek word for authority is 'exousia.' The definition below is from the NAS New Testament Greek Lexicon:

WISDOM TO DEFEAT THE ENEMY

Definition of authority:

Power of choice, liberty of doing as one pleases

Leave or permission

Physical and mental power

The ability or strength with which one is endued, which he either possesses or exercises

The power of authority(influence) and of right (privilege)

The power of rule or government (the power of him whose will and commands must be submitted to by others and obeyed)

Authority over mankind

The power of judicial decisions

Authority to manage domestic affairs

Jurisdiction

One who possesses authority

A ruler, a human magistrate

The leading and more powerful among created beings superior to man, spiritual potentates

A sign of the husband's authority over his wife

The veil with which propriety required a woman to cover herself

The sign of regal authority; a crown

This is your true identity in Christ! That is why scripture tells us in 1 John 4:4, "Greater is He that lives in me than he that is in the world." You've been given power and authority to reign and rule with Jesus. Jesus gave us His power and authority over every sickness, disease, and all kinds of spirits. He expects us to walk in the authority He gave us, having the confidence to continue to do the works of His ministry. Allow me to put this in a clearer explanation. If Jesus were speaking to you, this is what He would say:

"I trust you to do the works of the ministry. Even though you may feel inadequate or unsure of yourself at times, I have chosen to trust you with my delegated authority. My Spirit lives in You! Therefore, go do the works I've called you to, knowing I have commissioned you. I trust you to do what's right. You have the liberty to take decisive action. You are endued with supernatural strength by My Holy Spirit, which will enable you to accomplish My will and purpose. You have the right to exercise authority in My name because

I have given you the right to rule with governmental authority. You are royalty, and all of heaven will back you up.

This means that the enemy MUST SUBMIT to MY NAME. You have the right to make judicial decisions that will restore justice to the oppressed and manage domestic affairs. You have jurisdiction where I've placed you. You have the spiritual potency to bind the enemy and make him inoperable. I have set this seal of My ownership over you because you are a child of God. You have the authority to make a difference in the world around you. Use it well!"

Walking in obedience to God comes from a grateful heart, one who knows and appreciates how much they have been forgiven, but the word 'obey' in scripture is not optional. It's expected. A person can obey God without necessarily having a yielded heart; they simply do what they're told. Imagine a child that obeys what their parent tells them to do, but their heart is pouting and angry about it the whole time. Living in submission to God's Holy Spirit is entirely different. It is a humble yielding to the Lord's wishes, and it comes from knowing Him personally. Submission is a personal choice to honor God in all we do. Authority and power increase when we walk in compassion, faith, love, obedience, and humility.

Compassion is a conduit for miracles. Matt. 14:13-14; Matt.20:30-34; Luke 7:12-15; John 11:34-44.

Faith expresses itself through love. Gal. 5:6.

Faith moves mountains. Mark 11:22-24.

Obedience puts us in the right relationship with God. 1 Sam. 15:22. It also releases the blessings of God.

Gen. 22:17-18; Prov. 13:13; Luke 11:28.

God's grace and assistance comes to the humble. James 4:6, Prov. 22:4, 1 Pet. 5:6, Is. 66:2.

PRE-PRAYER EXERCISE

Breakthrough is not always the result of just saying the prayer; it comes with that 'aha' moment of revelation that hits your spirit with truth. The light of God's truth pierces the darkness so that the lies can no longer hold people in captivity. When the proverbial light bulb comes on in your mind and heart, the darkness has to flee!

Consider your own life and the ways the enemy has spoken his lies over you. As you have read through these pages, what areas seem to apply to you? What aspects of the orphan spirit and the poverty mindset are true for you? Write them down, or simply refer back to the charts for reference. These are areas that you should talk to God about during your prayer time. It is the sincere prayer from the heart that acknowledges areas of sin and shortcomings that connects your heart to God's and helps release you from the chains of captivity.

Practically speaking, faith without works is dead. Faith is not truly faith unless we take a step towards God. One way to break the poverty spirit is through sowing financially. Every person's situation is different. You may or may not belong to a local church, so where should you sow? Perhaps God is asking you to give into your local church, or it could be another ministry, a widow, or another struggling family. It is important to ask God where He wants you to sow your seed, because when we sow in obedience, that will be the ground anointed for a breakthrough.

Do not let your preconceived ideas, judgments, or criticisms hinder you from what God instructs you to do! Part of faith is listening, obeying, and acting on what we've heard, not reasoning with our natural mind. Let me give you a brief example. One day many years ago, a woman came into the bookstore where I was working and she looked troubled. I struck up a conversation with her, and she disclosed that she was having some financial difficulty to the point where it had become urgent. Her outward appearance was well-kept and well-dressed.

As a matter of fact, I couldn't help noticing that she had pulled up in a Lexus, and it was parked right in front of the store. I wrestled with what I saw in the natural and wondered if she was being dishonest, yet the inner witness of the Holy Spirit urged me to give her a love offering. As I pulled out my purse to write her a check, suddenly, two other customers who had overheard our conversation did the exact same thing. We each wrote this woman a check for $100. They, too, had the inner witness of the Holy Spirit impressing on their hearts to give. Our Father wanted us to help this woman. This is a good lesson not to judge by outward appearances, but to be led by the Spirit.

Giving is not just financial, but if you need a financial breakthrough, then you must sow finances. The kingdom of God is a backwards kingdom. In order to receive, you must first give. Look up the scriptures on giving. Seeds reproduce after their kind. If you need groceries, sow food, groceries, or a meal into someone else. You can sow your time, resources, talents, and even practical household items or a service you can offer, but the important thing is to develop a lifestyle of giving and generosity. When you do, you will set up a cycle of continuous sowing that will also reap continuous blessings that come back to you. These acts of faith will break the power of a poverty mentality in your life.

PRAYER

Heavenly Father,

I thank you for the revelation that will uproot any lies in my belief system. I ask You, Holy Spirit, to show me anything I need to understand so that I can be led into freedom. Expose the things the enemy has hidden so that the lies and agreements with the kingdom of darkness can be uprooted and removed in Jesus's name.

Satan, I divorce you. You are not my master, my spouse, and I will not serve you. I break all agreements that have been made by myself or my ancestors, knowingly or unknowingly, and I renounce any partnership, covenant, or contracts with Satan and any spirits under his control. I repent for any lies that I have believed. I submit myself to the authority of the Lord Jesus Christ, my heavenly Father, and the Holy Spirit. I thank You, Jesus, for dying my death on the cross, for taking the stripes so that I could live free and healed. I am glad to call you my Lord and Savior. I thank You for showing me the way back to my Father. I bind the following spirits in the name and authority of the Lord Jesus Christ:

_ The Spirit of Fear

_ The Orphan Spirit

_ Spirit of Rejection

_ Spirit of Broken Heart

_ Spirits of Loneliness and Isolation

_ Spirits of Jealousy, Rivalry, and Competition

_ Spirits of Unbelief, Double-Mindedness, Poverty, and Death

_ Spirits of Selfish Ambition, Comparison, and Envy

_ Spirit of Haughtiness and Pride

_ Spirits of Dishonor, Disapproval, and Disappointment

_ Spirits of Anger and Rage

_ Spirits of Bondage, Alcohol, Pharmacia, and Addiction

_ Spirits of Accusation, Criticism, and Judgment

_ Spirit of Unforgiveness and Bitterness

_ Spirits of Rebellion and Idolatry

_ Spirit of Confusion

_ Spirits of Mind-Binding and Octopus Spirits

_ Spirits of Self-Pity and Victim Spirit

_ Spirits of Shame, Guilt and Condemnation

_ Spirits of Past and Regret

_ Spirit of Python

_ Spirit of Heaviness

_ Spirits of Unloving and Unwanted

_ Spirits of Whoredom, Idolatry, and Witchcraft

_ All lying and familiar spirits

I command them to leave me now, to go back to hell and to remain there. Father, let Your angels be released to chain these spirits in the abyss until the day of their judgment. I thank you for forgiving me.

Father, I forgive my parents for not being able to meet my emotional needs. I forgive them for any fear, rejection, or feeling of abandonment that came in due to factors beyond my control. I forgive them for any form of neglect or abuse that caused me to grow up fearful, angry, or resentful towards authority. I forgive my parents (also name other family members if applicable) for breaking my trust and causing me to feel betrayed, hurt, rejected, unloved, unwanted, or the lie that I am somehow defective. I forgive any injustices that occurred that made me feel vulnerable, ashamed, inferior, and insecure, and I forgive my parents and family members for opening the door to the enemy. I repent for holding any negative judgments against them, and I release them from any debt I have felt they owed to me. I understand they, too, were broken and could not give me what they didn't have.

Father, I release the grief over the loss of the emotional bonding that I always longed for with my parents. I let go of the feelings of rejection, knowing that it was my parent's inability to love and nurture me, not anything I have done to create these feelings of unworthiness. That is their emotional deficit, and I don't have to own it. I refuse to reject myself any longer.

I renounce any ungodly or unhealthy soul ties to my mother and father (including any other family members that this may apply to), and I send all fragmented parts of their souls back to them. I call for any fragmented parts of my soul that are connected to them to come back to me. I put the blood of Jesus over every ungodly agreement and old covenant that the enemy is enforcing, and I declare the blood of Jesus voids all previous contracts. I declare I am planted in love, because I am 'in Christ.'

Lord, I have allowed anxiety, worry, and stress to rob me of peace and joy. I have accused you in my heart of things that You did not do. Forgive me for listening to the wrong voice and blaming You. Forgive me for striving and not being able to trust You in all things. Forgive me for not releasing my faith, for stinginess and selfishness. Forgive me for feeling like a victim and giving in to self-pity. Help me overcome a poverty mindset and live in the light and truth of Your word. Let Your Holy Spirit flood my heart with the revelation of Your love and acceptance for me. Let Your Holy Spirit reveal the Spirit of Adoption in my heart, so that I never feel like an orphan again. Bless me with the revelation that heals my heart from abandonment issues and reveals the heart of my Father towards me.

I confess that I am grateful for all that You have given me, and for all that You've already done for me, Jesus. I thank you for releasing a Spirit of Faith and Grace to me, that enables me to engage my faith with the truth of Your word, and live in a different reality than what I have experienced up to now. I thank You that You make all things new. I declare I am not an orphan. I am not unwanted or unloved. I am deeply valued and cherished by my Father. I am adopted into the family of God, and I am loved. I am royalty because I am a child of God. I don't have to fight or strive to be blessed. I am already blessed. My sins are forgiven and I have eternal life. Everything I will ever need has already been prepared for me. It is mine by faith. I simply need to rest in this truth.

I thank You for healing my brokenness, and leading me into good, healthy relationships where I can prosper and be in health. I thank you for the restoration of my emotions, relationships, and finances, and, most of all, for restoring me to my true identity. Help me to be generous, gracious, and forgiving towards others, to live a life that honors you. In Jesus's name, amen.

CHAPTER TWO
COMMON BLOCKS TO PRAYER

God uses all of our life experiences to create teachable moments. How often I have wanted my healing and freedom to come easily, and yet every part of my personal progress has seemed like being in a wrestling match with an alligator. God's processes don't involve shortcuts! He wants us to really learn His ways so that we can teach the truth to others. We must learn how these spirits communicate with us so that we can identify them in other people.

There are many times when people simply don't understand why their prayers are blocked or hindered for some reason, but I believe it comes from our own personal blind spots. Sometimes that comes from a lack of knowing God's word and spiritual realities, and other times it's simply because we know the truth but have failed to live in obedience to it. The following subsections in this chapter are dedicated to some of the most common blocks to prayer.

LACK OF CONFESSION & REPENTANCE

The Bible teaches that sin separates us from God. (ref. Is.59:2, Ps. 66:18). Yet, Jesus came to deal with our sin issue so that we could be restored to a relationship with God. There are various teachings in the body of Christ that include a 'once saved, always saved' theology, and that all our sin has already been forgiven; therefore, there is no need for ongoing confession or repentance. This is also part of a hyper-grace movement that is a dangerous deception. How do we resolve the apparent contradiction? Is there a need to ask for forgiveness of sin?

Jesus taught repentance. (Mt. 4:17; Lk. 13). His teaching pointed out the importance of repentance so that people did not die outside of God's grace and care. The way people avoided being caught 'off guard' at an unexpected moment of death was through trusting their souls to the great physician, Jesus. In the same conversation and spiritual teaching, he also spoke on the parable of the fig tree (ref. Luke 13:6).

"A certain man had a fig tree planted in his vineyard, and he came seeking fruit on it and found none. Then he said to the keeper of his vineyard, 'Look, for three years, I have come seeking fruit on this fig tree and find none. Cut it down. Why does it use up the ground?'" "But he answered and said to him, 'Sir, let it alone this year also, until I dig around it and fertilize it. And if it bears fruit, *well*. But if not, after that you can cut it down.'"

The reference of believers, comparing them to the imagery of trees, is used in many places in scripture. These trees are intended to be objects of beauty, strength, and fruitfulness because they are the planting of the Lord. The fruit and leaves are intended to be healing to the nations. Anything that prevents the intended end of bringing glory to God, is viewed as undesirable in the life of the tree (also the life of the believer). Jesus said in John 15:1,

"I am the true vine, and My Father is the vinedresser. Every branch in Me that does not bear fruit He takes away: and every branch that bears fruit He prunes, that it may bear more fruit. You are already clean because of the word which I have spoken to you. Abide in Me, and I in you. As the branch cannot bear fruit of itself, unless it abides in the vine, neither can you, unless you abide in Me."

We are cleansed by the word of God so that we can bring forth good fruit and display holiness in our life. Jesus continued his teaching in the following comments in John 15:5-10, emphasizing the importance of abiding – or, in other words, obedience – that keeps the believer in the right relationship with God. Jesus made the connection between repentance and fruitfulness, *and,* the lack of repentance and how it hinders spiritual growth, fruitfulness, and maturity. A Christian that fails to recognize the importance of repentance also fails to recognize their own need for cleansing.

When we first came to Christ, we sought to have forgiveness and cleansing of all the sins we had committed up to the point of our salvation. Christ's death on the cross was to grant us mercy and forgiveness for every sin we had committed and would commit during our lives. The grace is available, however, we each still need to work out our salvation with fear and trembling before the Lord (ref. Phil. 2:12). Colossians 2:14 teaches us that Jesus canceled the debt of legal demands that were against us by nailing it to the cross. The sins that we committed before we were born again were wiped away, but sometimes people feel that grace is like a free pass to live as they please. Acknowledging our sins and shortcomings is an important part of maintaining the right relationship with God. If asking for forgiveness is not necessary, then the Bible would not speak on that matter.

1 John 1:8-10   "If we say we have no sin then we deceive ourselves and the truth is not in us. If we confess our sins, He is faithful and just to forgive our sins and cleanse us from all unrighteousness. If we say we have not sinned, we make Him out to be a liar and His word is not in us."

Prov. 28:13   "He who conceals his transgressions will not prosper, but he who confesses and forsakes them will find compassion."

Ps. 32:5   "Then I acknowledged my sin to You and did not hide my iniquity. I said, "I will confess my transgressions to the Lord, and You forgave the guilt of my sin.""

How can a person be forgiven of sins that they haven't yet committed? It makes sense, then, that when we commit sins, that is when we ask for forgiveness. The Bible is also clear that we will not prosper unless we receive cleansing from sin and iniquity. Under the New Covenant of grace, we have access to God's abundant mercy and restoration, but restoration always depends on repentance, cleansing, and obedience. If we allow unconfessed sin to build up, then the enemy has legal grounds to block our prayers from being answered.

God is a good Father. If one of his children is caught in disobedience, yet still asking for a prayer to be answered, He has the right to make a judgment call on when the prayer will be answered. He can say no or delay the answer until His child modifies their behavior. Grace is not a replacement for obedience. Real faith produces obedience, humility, and a submitted heart towards God. If we want to prosper and be in health, then it is important to know the truth of scripture and what is expected of us. Carelessness in this area, or failing to make a commitment to our own spiritual growth, leaves us vulnerable to the enemy.

THE EXISTENCE OF GENERATIONAL CURSES

There is a lot that can fall under personal and family sins. We may or may not be responsible for opening the door to certain sins, but it is our responsibility to renounce and forsake the sins that have been in our family line. The existence of unbroken curses is a common block to prayer because many people are unaware they exist, or they lack knowledge of how to break the curse.

Ezekiel 18:20 makes it clear that God is not applying the guilt of the parents' sin upon the children. However, parents that set an example of a sinful lifestyle can expect their children to also follow some of those same sinful behaviors. The parents have definitely contributed to whatever effects their sin has on their children and future generations, but it is the righteousness of each individual that releases their deliverance. Generational curses are sins and negative behavior that is repeated and passed down from one generation to another.

For instance, alcoholism or other addictions, lust, incest, mental illness, inherited diseases, untimely death, or witchcraft, to name a few, runs in certain families. These are things that are not just caused by natural occurrences such as learned behavior, but as a result of demonic spirits that bring defilement and enforce curses. Please note that when a person becomes born again as a child of God, it is NOT God that enforces the curse. It is the enemy, because he still finds legal grounds to do so.

Salvation is not the same issue as deliverance. Before we were born again and placed in a covenant with God, we were in a covenant with Satan and the spirits of darkness. Salvation transports us out of the covenant we had with darkness and into the kingdom of light. However, we must still do something intentional to cut off and cast out the familiar spirits that have been assigned to us and our families. **Familiar** means we know them, and certain behaviors have become habits. When someone repeatedly lies, for instance, it is an invitation for demonic spirits to take control of the person's tongue so that lying becomes habitual. It could be the same thing with drinking or using drugs or something else. Every time the person resorts to that behavior, demonic spirits gain strength in the person's life, binding them to that sin until the person finds themselves with an addiction they don't know how to break. They need the power of God to break the grip of Satan in their life.

Familial spirits (spirits that travel in certain families) are there first of all simply because no one told them to leave. These are spirits that are assigned to reproduce certain sins in a family. It could be anything from divorce, adultery, murder, rage, or something else. Secondly, those spirits are there to tempt other family members into repeating the same sins as their ancestors, so that they continue to have legal grounds to stay and enforce a curse. Getting saved does not automatically deliver a person from demonic attachments.

That is why we incorporate prayers of renouncement. They serve as a 'divorce decree,' putting the enemy on notice that any agreements, contracts or covenants that were made in the spiritual realm (either knowingly or unknowingly, by ourselves or our ancestors) - are now broken. The blood of Jesus is applied to atone for those sins. We apply the blood of Jesus to the covenants the enemy has had against us, and ask that our names be removed from ungodly altars. People don't stop to think about it, but when they sin, they offer Satan a form of worship. Repeated sin, even if it is something habitual like cursing, swearing, gossiping, slander or lying, actually begins to build an altar to the enemy. Whatever we do offers either glory to God or glory to the enemy.

Prov. 26:2   "Like a fluttering sparrow or a darting swallow, an underserved curse does not come to rest ..." (Berean Study Bible).

If the evidence of a curse exists, such as generational poverty, rebellion and stubbornness towards God, broken relationships and divorce, adultery, a life of worldliness and fornication, untimely death, addictions, and other forms of bondage, to name a few, then the enemy has found legal grounds to enforce it. It doesn't matter if it's considered generational or not; the proof is in the fruit. The enforcement of a curse can come through familiar spirits and other demonic attachments. They are assigned to us to hinder our progress, steal our blessings, and attempt to recreate, over and over again, the circumstances that give them legal grounds to stay in a person's life. These are agreements in the spiritual realm that serve as a contract or covenant with demons.

In the Old Testament, God warned His people not to serve other gods because that was a violation of His commands.

Exodus 20:2-3   "I am the Lord your God, who brought you out of Egypt, out of the land of slavery. You shall have no other gods before me." This was a warning against idolatry. The penalty was imposed for breaking His commands:

Exodus 20:5   "Thou shalt not bow down thyself to them, nor serve them: for I the LORD thy God [am] a jealous God, visiting the iniquity of the fathers upon the children unto the third and fourth [generation] of them that hate me;" KJV.

Num. 14:18   "The LORD [is] longsuffering, and of great mercy, forgiving iniquity and transgression, and by no means clearing [the guilty], visiting the iniquity of the fathers upon the children unto the third and fourth [generation]." A spiritual defilement took place due to disobedience, incurring the penalty of a curse.

Deut. 28   I won't quote all of it, but there were blessings for obedience; curses were imposed for disobedience. In Deut. 27: 14-26, Moses had the Levites read the penalties that would come upon the people if they disobeyed.

Curses for idolatry resulted in miscarriage, barrenness, loss of provision, confusion, mental health issues, sickness and disease, blindness, and ruin (ref. Deut. 28). God would not hear their prayer unless it was a prayer of repentance. Blessings of worshiping and serving God were the promise of fruitfulness. God would remove sickness from their midst, and their provision would be sure. (ref. Ex. 23:26).

In Deut. 28, the blessings were listed first because it is always God's desire to bless, show mercy and be gracious to His people. However, He is bound by His word. If we live in obedience, we receive blessings; if people are in disobedience, then they incur a curse, or, in other words, a loss of blessing. The curses were imposed; the effect of them became increasingly severe if repentance did not occur. Deut. 28:23 also declares a curse on agriculture and on the land. It becomes unproductive. See also Jeremiah 23:10, Lev. 18:24-27, Num. 35:33, 2 Sam. 21:1-14, 1 Kings 8:35, 2 Chron. 6:26.

The curse shuts up the heavens so that prayers cannot go through, either upwards towards God nor answered prayer coming down. Is. 59:2, Is. 1:15, Ezek. 39:23, Prov. 15:29, Jer. 5:25.

 The only prayer that can go through is the prayer of repentance. 2 Chron. 6:24-27; 2 Chron.7:14, 1 John 1:9. James 5:15,16.

In the Old Testament, God gave us a picture of actual events that symbolize spiritual principles. In the New Testament, Jesus won us the victory at the cross, but we must still appropriate that victory. This means doing something intentional to cooperate with God in our deliverance to demonstrate repentance. **God's blessings are released upon our obedience!**

In the Old Testament, the spiritual leaders told the people God's laws, then had them renounce the sins of their ancestors. Ex. Lev. 26:40-41, Lev. 5:5, 1 Kings 8:33, Ezra 10:1-11, Daniel 9:1-21, Dan. 10:12, Neh. 1:6.

Other scripture examples of confession and repentance are: 1 Kings 8:30, Hosea 5:15, Is. 58:9, Is. 65:24, Ps. 32:5, Ps. 51:2, Ps. 145:18, 1 John 1:8-9, Prov. 28:13.

New Testament: Christ won the victory for us by becoming our substitute on the cross. He took the penalty of our sins upon Himself so that we could live free.

Gal. 3:13   "Christ hath redeemed us from the curse of the law, being made a curse for us: for it is written, Cursed [is] every one that hangeth on a tree" KJV.

Gal. 3:10   "Listen, whoever seeks to be righteous by following certain works of the law actually falls under the law's curse. I'm giving it to you straight from Scripture because it is as true now as when it was written: "Cursed is everyone who doesn't live by and do all that is written in the law."(VOICE Translation)

We see that the spiritual principles of confession and repentance are consistent throughout scripture. Of course, everything in the Old Testament is weighed against the cross of Christ. The word 'curse' is not necessarily used as much in the New Testament, but the principles of confession and repentance in order to receive cleansing and atonement (the application of the blood) remain. When there is a lack of blessing, it is an indication of spiritual blockage or a curse.

God never changed His mind about obedience, and He didn't wipe out the consequences of disobedience just because we are under grace. We must still do our part, or we leave ourselves vulnerable to the enemy. The enemy must have our cooperation or find a place of agreement. Repentance and prayers of renouncement help break demonic attachments and remove the legal grounds the enemy uses against God's people so that the curse can no longer be enforced.

My suggestion is to get a notebook and begin to write any areas that you are aware of in your personal family that may signify a repeated pattern or area of sin that could be considered a curse. Whether it's generational or not, it will need to be addressed in prayer.

Ask Holy Spirit to bring to mind things you may have forgotten about. Ask family members to help you identify any skeletons in the closet in your family history.

Emotional & Mental Health Issues

Depression, Bi-polar, Schizophrenia, Self-Rejection, Self-Hatred, Neglect, Verbal Outbursts, Toxic Shame, Suicidal thoughts & behaviors, Narcissism, Nightmares, Obsessive-Compulsive behaviors, Abusing oneself (self-harm), Depraved thoughts.

Sins of Anger

Uncontrollable fits of anger or rage, Violent actions or feels tendencies towards violence on the inside, Aggression, Any form of abuse, Desire for revenge, Unforgiveness, Bitterness, Brawling, Hatred, Sins of the mouth (slander, character assassination, malicious gossip).

Evil Speaking

Gossip, Slander, Lying, Cursing and swearing, Complaining, Being Contentious or Argumentative, Verbal abuse, Exaggeration, Mocking God, Backbiting, Blasphemy, Boasting, Ridiculing others, Divisiveness, and Separating friendships.

Substance Abuse & Addictions

Food addictions, Bulimia, Anorexia, Abuse of prescription medications, Alcohol, and drug abuse, Tobacco, Gambling, and Sex addictions.

Sexual Sins

Fornication, Lust, Pornography, Masturbation, Homosexuality, Bi-sexuality, Orgies, Rape, Perversion, Incest, Gender identity confusion, Transvestite, Bestiality, Pedophilia, Voyeurism, Ungodly fantasies, Incubus/Succubus (Sexual Spirits).

False Religions, Cults & Secret Societies

Hinduism & Yoga, Kundalini Worship, Buddism, Islam, Mormonism, Bahaism, Rosicrucianism Scottish Rite, Shriners, Catholicism, Santeria, Voodoo, Freemasonry, Klu Klux Klan, White Supremacy, Scientology, Illuminati, Wicca and Witchcraft, Satanism, Luciferian and other occult religions. Spiritual abuse, Satanic Ritual Abuse, MK Ultra, Legalism, Jehovah's Witness, Mormonism, Buddhism, False doctrines, False Religions, Masonic Lodges, Freemasonry.

Occult Involvement

Casting Spells, Incantations, Charms and Hexes, Word Curses, Psychics, Fortune-Telling, Mediums, Seances, Conjuring Spirits, Channeling spirits, Palm Reading, Divination, Water Witching, Ouija board, Bloody Mary Games, Occult Games, Magic 8 Ball (A Form of Divination), Telepathy, Hypnotism, Astral Projection & Out-of-Body Experiences, Invoking/Praying to Saints, Levitation, Tarot Cards, Palm Readings, Consulting Mediums, Mysticism and New Age/Eastern Religions, Hinduism, Bahaism, Native American Spirit Worship, Spirit Guides, Hare Krishna, Mormonism, Islam and the Worship of Allah, Rosicrucianism, Idolatry: (Money, Sex, Power, Position & Titles, Self-Worship, etc,)Reiki Healing, Unholy Mass & Unholy Communion, Bloodshed and Blood Ceremonies, Cannibalism, Mock Ceremonies, Human and Animal Sacrifice, Ungodly Vows, Covenants and Offerings to Demonic Spirits, Pagan Rituals and Traditions, Rape, Violence, Demonic Tattoos, Astrology, Horoscopes, MK Ultra Mind Control, Numerology, Angel Worship, Celebrating All Saints Day, Day of the Dead, Building Altars and Shrines, Celebration of Santa Muerte.

Sins of Dishonesty

Craftiness, Defrauding, Deceit, Lying, Double-tongued, Insincere Conversation, Bearing False Witness, False Submission, Walking in False Authority, Hypocrisy & Pretense, False Repentance.

Envy & Jealousy

Covetousness, Having an evil eye or Selfish motives, Lusting for material items, Desire for superiority over others.

Enjoying the Company of Sinners

Drunkenness, Debauchery, Orgies, Haters of God, Mocking God, Contriving Evil, Carnal Pleasures, Homosexuality, Forbidden sexual sins, Lovers of self (idolatry).

Sins of Pride

High-mindedness, Unrepentant, Self-importance, Obstinate/Stubborn, Arrogance, Self-willed, Rebellious, Self-promoting, Selfish ambition, Seditions (stirring up people against authority), Speaking ill of others, Stirring up strife, Quarrelsome, Speaking against the Holy Spirit, Blame Shifting, Refusing to take responsibility for one's faults, Accusation.

Critical Spirit

Fault-Finding, Judgementalism, Self-Righteousness, Belittling others, Shaming others, Coarse Joking, Shunning, Rejection, and Bullying spirit.

Fears

Insecurity, Inferiority, Constant questioning of God's word, Fear of Man, Cowardice, and Anxiety (fears are rooted in unbelief towards God and lack of faith towards God).

Possessiveness

Covetousness, Controlling, Manipulative, Jealousy, Greed, Hoarding, Stealing, Stinginess.

Rebellion

Stubbornness, Pride, Arrogance, Controlling behaviors, Witchcraft, Idolatry, Lawlessness, Disobedience, Defiance towards Authority, Anti-Christ, Racism, Fornication, and Self-Deception.

Victim Mentality

Self-Pity, Attention Seeker, Blame Shifting, Narcissism, Co-Dependency, Defeated Attitude, Hopelessness, Feelings of Entitlement, Emotional Paralysis, Unworthiness, Expects Failure, Pessimist, Unbelieving.

Covenant Breaker

Broken Vows and Divorce, Adultery, Promise-Breaker, Broken Agreements, Untrustworthy.

Make sure you write down everything that you know is true for yourself or your ancestors, then methodically go through and renounce them. You can find a very thorough Breakthrough Prayer at Xpect A Miracle Ministries, under the pages section: It is the Breakthrough Prayer. There is another link, also under the pages section, called Prayers and Decrees to Open the Heavens and Bring Revival.

I have also included a prayer at the end of each sub-section. The first one deals with inherited generational curses.

PRAYER

Dear Heavenly Father,

I come to You on behalf of myself and all those in my ancestral line that came before me. I ask for Your forgiveness for our sins, and I acknowledge that many of us never asked for Jesus Christ to be our Lord and Savior. Many of us committed sins and trespassed in rebellion to Your ways.

Father, I also come to you as a citizen of the United States, and I ask You to forgive the sins of our forefathers. I ask You to forgive the sins of those that pioneered and settled this land and the pagan practices, cultures, and traditions brought in from foreign lands. Forgive, I pray, our presidential and political leaders that broke treaties and treacherously removed the boundary lines of Native Americans and others to claim them as their own.

Forgive all those in my family line, as well as those who founded our nation and settled the land for making slaves of other races and nationalities; for causing others to feel overcome with jealousy, fear, anger, and desire vengeance against those who treated them wrongfully.

Forgive us for the grief we caused, the injustices, and the bloodshed. Forgive us for broken covenants, vows, and agreements and for the curses that came as a result of those actions. Although I may not have personally taken part in these sins, I understand that there is a need to recognize the sins of those that came before us, and I ask for the blood of Jesus to atone for these things so that we may be cleansed of all these unrighteous acts. Please allow all those that have been affected by a generational root of bitterness, grief, and poverty, to now find the grace to forgive generations of mistreatment and injustices.

Father, You said that if I would humble myself, pray and seek Your face... If I would turn and repent from my wicked ways, You said You would forgive my sins. Whether me or my family members have partaken of these sins knowingly or unknowingly, I ask Your forgiveness for generational rebellion, idolatry, serving false gods and masters, murder and sins of innocent bloodshed, evil speaking, cursing God and others, sexual immorality, adultery, broken vows and covenants, lying, failing to love others, sins of selfishness and greed, stealing, taking the name of the Lord in vain, failing to honor and respect my parents and other authority figures, bearing false witness and breaking other commandments.

Forgive us for our sins and wash us clean by the blood that You shed for us, Lord Jesus. I invite You to be my Lord and Savior, and I thank You for dying in my place on the cross. I believe You are the Son of God and that You can break the power of sin in my life. Thank you for eternal life and for helping me to know how to have a relationship with the living God. In Jesus's name, amen.

UNFORGIVENESS & BITTERNESS

Unforgiveness is by far the most common block to prayer. It's a funny thing about forgiveness. A person can tell themselves they have forgiven someone and try to convince themselves they have forgiven, when the reality is their heart doesn't witness that is the truth. When the heart remains unconvinced, the matter is not yet settled.

How does one arrive at true forgiveness and know that it is not just us trying to convince ourselves, but in fact, a genuine act of divine intervention, allowing us to genuinely forgive someone that has sinned against us? A person can go through the same process (sometimes for years) of confessing from their mouth, "Lord, I forgive so-and-so" for what they did; they can even try to convince God that they have forgiven. Sometimes a person can declare it to be so, yet still miss the boat.

When it seems that all your efforts fail to release your heart from the struggle, what is required is both willingness on your part and divine intervention on the part of God. He never asks us to do something that He does not give us His help to carry out. Jesus said we must forgive others, or God cannot forgive us of our own sins, but He does not leave us without His help. He provides the grace to pull those stubborn weeds out of wounded, bitter hearts so that His love and grace will flow from vessels of integrity.

Until you see the offender in the light of your own human weakness and can bring yourself to identify with them as a person who has been wounded, genuine forgiveness will escape you. It is when we can accept the fact that the person who did wrong to us did so out of their own unresolved pain, perhaps their own fears or insecurities, and we are just as prone to making the same type of error if perhaps we had felt what they experienced.

What would have happened if we had heard the enemy's logic as it had been whispered in their ears? How would we have reacted if we had felt the same emotions, listened to the enemy's twisted ideas of truth, and become prey to be used for wrongdoing? Could it be possible that we would have committed the same type of fault? Have we ever done something similar in times past, perhaps never stopping to think that we, too, were once guilty of a similar offense?

I know that there are some things that are just plain heinous. There are unthinkable things that predators have done to willfully harm others. Yet, they, too, were once just children. Innocents that had something inexplicable or perhaps unimaginable done to them. The wounded, if they are never healed, go on to become predators themselves, lashing out to hurt and offend others or willfully mistreat them. It doesn't excuse wrong behavior, but it helps us understand it. It is truly only God's grace that can intervene and allow us to see deep hurt and offense in this light. It is the piercing light of His love that allows compassion to arise, enabling us to forgive those that have hurt us. This is the divine gift of God's grace, to forgive with genuine humility of heart. When your heart has truly released the person that offended you, you will feel your heart soften towards them. You will experience the gift of compassion that allows you to be forever free from those old wounds.

It doesn't necessarily mean that the person we have forgiven is off the hook with God, but it means that we are. If we are to ever recover real joy and peace, we must ask God for His ability to see the perpetrators through His eyes, for in doing so, He also grants His ability to forgive. It comes from understanding all human beings, no matter how grave their sin and faults, are prone to being used by the enemy to inflict pain onto others – as we all have been at one time or another.

It was for this reason that God sent His only Son, Jesus Christ, to walk among man and demonstrate Divine Love and Grace. Intellectually we may know this to be true and accept the word of God. But until we model it … live it … demonstrate it … we fall tremendously short of being Christ-like. God gives us challenges with human relationships not so that we can dwell upon the pain, but so that we have endless opportunities to demonstrate that we truly KNOW Him.

Unresolved unforgiveness will grow into a root of bitterness, and bitterness is directly related to witchcraft and rebellion. A root of bitterness can be passed down as a generational curse. All bitterness is connected to the spirit of witchcraft and rebellion.

1 Sam. 15:23   "For rebellion is as the sin of divination and insubordination is as the sin of iniquity and idolatry."

Bitterness *is as* rebellion, which is the root of all witchcraft. Stubbornness *is as* idolatry. Bitterness, which comes from unresolved unforgiveness, is equated with the same sort of sin as rebellion, and stubbornness (the willful resistance to obedience) is the same as making ourselves our own god (the sin of idolatry). Idolatry, witchcraft, and rebellion receive penalties of the curse.

Retaining offense, holding on to negative judgments toward others, and being critical with the mouth are all indicators of a heart that is not free nor healed. Unforgiveness opens the door to torment, which can come in the form of tormenting thoughts (rehearsing the wrongs others have done to us), lack of peace, torment in the body (physical illness, ulcers, gallbladder issues, back problems (which speaks of alignment issues) and other 'tormenting pains'; it can also become the root cause of diseases such as cancer, mental illness and other issues that affect the health of the body. The prefix *'dis'* means 'not' or 'opposite of, also 'come apart.' So, disease essentially means *not peace*, or the opposite of peace. The opposite of peace is torment, confusion, fear, and anxiety. The lack of peace or *dis*-ease leads to disease of the physical body.

Unforgiveness blocks a person's ability to hear from God and connect with His Holy Spirit. It can lead to feelings of being rejected by God because the person is unable to feel, sense, or hear from the Lord until the unforgiveness is dealt with. (ref Matthew 18:1-33.). The reality is the individual is not rejected by God but is under discipline for their lack of obedience. The demonic tormenters are present to motivate the person back to the right behavior and a restored relationship with God. Obedience to God's word removes the legal grounds the enemy seeks to use against people, and the block to prayer is eliminated. Many times, when the emotional issues of holding unforgiveness towards someone is released, the answered prayer for physical healing (or another petition) can then be answered

Matt. 5:22-24   "But I say to you that everyone who is angry with his brother will be guilty before the court, and whoever says to his brother 'You good for nothing' shall be guilty before the supreme court; and whoever says 'You fool' shall be guilty enough to go into the fiery hell. Therefore, if you are presenting your offering at the altar and there remember that your brother has something against you, leave your gift there before the altar and go. First be reconciled to your brother, and then come and offer your gift." NASB

Matt. 6:14   "For if you forgive others their trespasses, your heavenly Father will also forgive you."

1 Cor. 13:4-7   "Love is patient and kind; love does not envy or boast; it is not arrogant or rude. It does not insist on its own way; it is not irritable or resentful; it does not rejoice at wrongdoing,

but rejoices with the truth. Love bears all things, believes all things, hopes all things, endures all things."

Gal. 6:1-2   "Brothers, if anyone is caught in any transgression, you who are spiritual should restore him in a spirit of gentleness. Keep watch on yourself, lest you too be tempted."

Bitterness also **produces barrenness** because bitterness involves contempt. King David's wife, Michal, despised David's worship. She was embarrassed by the King's utter abandonment in worship and had the audacity to disregard the importance of God's presence in her husband's life. She didn't stop to consider the significance of her defiance towards God and her snobbery towards both God and King David. As a result of her offensive behavior, Michal was sent away and never had intimacy with King David again. She was barren from that day forth. Michal's attitude of lightly esteeming the presence of God and her attempt to quench the Spirit is an example to all of us today, and also a warning not to treat the presence of the Holy Spirit with casual disregard.

2 Sam. 6:20-23   "When David returned home to bless his household, Michal daughter of Saul came out to meet him and said, "How the king of Israel has distinguished himself today, going around half-naked in full view of the slave girls of his servants as any vulgar fellow would!" David said to Michal, "It was before the Lord, who chose me rather than your father or anyone from his house when he appointed me ruler over the Lord's people Israel—I will celebrate before the Lord. I will become even more undignified than this, and I will be humiliated in my own eyes. But by these slave girls you spoke of, I will be held in honor." And Michal, daughter of Saul, had no children to the day of her death.

1 Sam. 2:30   "Therefore, the LORD, the God of Israel, declares: 'I did indeed say that your house and the house of your father would walk before Me forever. But now the LORD declares: Far be it from Me! For I will honor those who honor Me, but those who despise Me will be disdained." Berean Study Bible.

Many churches, ministries, and individuals are barren because they have offended and quenched the Holy Spirit. We cannot birth without the flow of the anointing, and the anointing comes from the Holy Spirit. Holy Spirit is the one that brings things to birth! Not by might, nor by power but by HIS Spirit! God never births anything new through a spirit of **bitterness** because it **is a defiling spirit,** and it **quenches** the Holy Spirit. Bitterness is aligned with rebellion, and rebellion is the root of all witchcraft (ref. 1 Sam. 15:23; Heb. 12:15; Acts 8:23).

PRAYER

Father God,

I thank You for showing me anyone I might still need to forgive. Bring their name to mind, Lord. I want to please You, so I ask You to give me the gift of Divine Grace. I ask You to enable me to see those that have hurt or offended me through Your eyes.

Help me to stop blaming them for things that have gone wrong in my life or how their behavior hurt and offended me. I realize that their character deficit belongs to them, and I don't have to own it any longer. Help me to have compassion on them so that I can truly forgive and be healed. I choose to do what is right in your eyes, Father. I yield my heart to the authority of your Holy Spirit, and I give you permission to uproot any stubborn spirit or attitude that tries to manipulate my emotions.

Holy Spirit, you may change my mind and change my responses so that the enemy does not triumph over me. I forgive (insert names), and I ask You to bless them however You want to bless them. I let go of any negative judgments, and I cancel their debt. Let the blood of Jesus cover their sin and mine, and cleanse us from all unrighteousness. Forgive me, too, Lord, for I need Your forgiveness and Your mercy every day.

Holy Spirit, I also ask You to forgive me for any ways that I have shown contempt or casual disregard for Your presence in my life, in the life of others, or in my house of worship. Forgive me for grieving You, quenching Your Spirit, or dishonoring You. Please don't take Your Holy Spirit from me. Create in me a clean heart, O God, and let my ways be pleasing to You. In Jesus's name, amen.

UNBELIEF & DOUBLE-MINDEDNESS

When prayers are hindered by unbelief, doubt, and double-mindedness, prayers go unanswered simply because we are not in alignment with faith. Scripture tells us,

Heb. 11:6	"And it is impossible to please God without faith. Anyone who wants to come to him must believe that God exists and that he rewards those who sincerely seek him."
Mark 6:5-6	"And he could do no mighty work there, except that he laid his hands on a few sick people and healed them. And he marveled because of their unbelief" ESV.
James 1:6-8	"But he must ask in faith, without doubting, because he who doubts is like a wave of the sea, blown and tossed by the wind. That man should not expect to receive anything from the Lord. He is a double-minded man, unstable in all his ways … " Berean Study Bible.

Unbelief, due to a spirit of familiarity, bound Jesus from being able to do mighty works in his hometown. God will most often work through people already in our lives, but the danger is in developing unbelief towards the anointing they carry due to familiarity. Have you disqualified someone from being a powerful and effective vessel of the Lord because you know them? Sometimes people approach the word of God like that, too. Our ears and minds get dull because we don't come to the word of God with any sense of expectancy that He will speak. Sometimes it is what you think you already know that blocks your ability to receive.

PRAYER

Father God,

I repent for any attitude that is rooted in unbelief. I know that it takes faith to please You. I ask Your forgiveness for looking at natural circumstances and receiving those things as reality rather than taking Your word as truth. I also repent for any way that I have broken faith in you and believed the lies of the enemy. I apologize to You for judging other servants of the Lord and discounting the work of grace You have done in their lives simply because they are familiar to me. Forgive me if you have wanted to minister to me through people that I disqualified in my own mind because I knew too much about them, or saw them after their past. I repent for my pride. I would not want others to disqualify me simply because they know me. I apologize, Holy Spirit, for grieving you by judging others and discounting Your power and authority working in other vessels. Forgive me, Father, for any agreements that I've made, knowingly or unknowingly, that have placed me in agreement with doubt, double-mindedness, or unbelief. Let the blood of Jesus cover my sin. In Jesus's name, amen.

TRYING TO BYPASS THE CONSEQUENCES OF DISOBEDIENCE

The spirit realm understands when we are not truly submitted to the authority of God in our life, and it grants demons legal grounds to withstand our prayers. Sometimes people want to receive an answer to prayer, but they are not committed to walking in obedience to God's word. We already discussed certain examples, such as holding on to unforgiveness or the laws of sowing and reaping. What we sow will always come back to us, whether it's positive or negative. The following examples cite some of the reasons why God does not answer, or prayers are blocked:

The individual has set themselves up to be an enemy or an adversary to the saints of God (Ps. 18:40-41; Hab. 1:13; Is. 57:11; Ps. 50:20-22).

Practicing evil and oppression towards others (Micah 3:2-4; Prov. 6:12-19; Ps. 34:15).

Guilty of shedding blood/murderous intent (Is. 1:15; Isaiah 59:3; Matt. 15:18-20; Eccl. 27:15).

Guilty of idolatry (Luke 16:13; Ezek. 14:1-11; Matt.6:21-23,33; Ezek. 8:15-18).

Guilty of hypocrisy (Matt.22:18; Rom.2:1-5; Luke 12:1; 1 John 2:4).

Pride. A proud heart is not submitted to God (James 4: 5-6; Eccl. 21:4; Eccl. 51:10; Prov. 8:13).

Sin and Iniquity (Jer. 21:2; Ps.66:18; Is. 59:2; John 9:31).

Departing from God (1 Sam. 28:6-7).

Deaf to the cry of the poor (Deut. 15:7-11; Prov. 21:13; Prov. 28:27).

Ignoring God's wisdom (Prov. 1:24-30; Prov.3:31-34).

Despising correction and hating instruction are signs of rebellion against God (Prov. 5:11-13).

PRAYER

Dear Heavenly Father,

I ask Your forgiveness for asking you to answer my prayer when I've been in violation of Your word. Forgive me for my disobedience. On behalf of myself and my ancestors, I repent for any ways that we have not walked in love towards others and have acted as an adversary instead, especially to those that are my brothers and sisters in the Lord.

I repent for any ways that we, especially myself, have practiced evil (be specific) or have acted as an oppressor toward others. Forgive us for bloodshed and sins of murder, including character assassination, which is murder with the mouth. Forgive us for carrying hatred in our hearts.

Forgive us for sins of idolatry, pride, and arrogance. Forgive us for hypocrisy, rebellion, and despising correction. I'm sorry for all the ways that I and those in my family line departed from You and didn't continue in fellowship with You. Forgive us for ignoring Your wisdom and inviting destruction into our lives. Forgive us for ignoring the cries of others when it was in our power to help and make a difference. There have been many ways that we have incurred guilt. Help me to walk in ways that are pleasing to You, Father. Please let the blood of Jesus cover my sin and iniquities and wash away the stench of sin, in Jesus's name, amen.

ASKING WITH WRONG INTENT (SELFISHNESS)

Prayers are not answered because of selfish ambition, motivated by the lust of the world, or misplaced priorities (James 4:3; Prov. 16:2; Prov. 21:2).

PRAYER

Father,

Forgive me for praying with selfish intent. I repent for envy, self-seeking and selfish ambition. Forgive me for striving and trying to prove my worth to myself or others. Forgive me for being driven by insecurity, inferiority, toxic shame, and perfectionism rather than trusting what You have to say about me. Forgive me for trying to impress others instead of trusting my relationship with You to impute value to me. The world cannot impute value, self-worth, or a sense of identity; only You can do that for me. Holy Spirit, turn the internal switch off that drives me. Let me instead be led by Your Spirit. Deliver me from fear and anxiety, rejection, and a sense of trying to overcome the disapproval of others and disapproval towards myself. I repent for being filled with lust and asking for things with the wrong priorities. I yield to You, father. I thank You for Your forgiveness, in Jesus's name.

ASKING OUTSIDE OF GOD'S WILL

There are some things that are subject to God's sovereign will. We always believe it is His will to heal and restore, but sometimes God has a different plan. Don't assume you know what it is; ask God if what you are praying for is His will before you proceed. Otherwise, you could end up asking for something outside of His will.

Prayers The son that was conceived in sin was not spared. David took Uriah's life and must be according to the will of God. 1 John 5:14-15.

PRAYER

Father God,

I repent for any ways that I have prayed for things outside of Your will, or insisted on trying to force my will to come to pass. If I have prayed for things that are actually fighting against Your will, please show me. Help me to release any prayer burdens that are not of you. Help me be confident of Your will by finding out what Your word has to say, rather than leaning on my own understanding.

Help me not to lean on my own understanding or to presume that I know Your will. You are sovereign, and You are aware of details that I am not. Forgive me if I have prayed for things not in accordance to Your will. I ask You to give me clarity in specific situations where I may be unsure, and to lead me to the correct scriptures that will help settle the matter in question. I pray for You to show me by Your Spirit how and what to pray according to Your will. I break any agreement I have made knowingly or unknowingly with the spirit of witchcraft, control, lying spirits and self-deception, and the spirit of error. Please let the blood of Jesus cover these sins and close the door to the enemy. In Jesus's name, amen.

OUTSIDE OF FELLOWSHIP WITH THE FATHER

Sin breaks our relationship with our Father. It also produces a guilty conscience, and those with a guilty conscience usually avoid fellowship with those that are living righteously because they are afraid of exposure. They often avoid God as well because they are enjoying the pleasures of sin and trying to avoid the conviction of the Holy Spirit. This puts people outside of fellowship with their Father. Scriptures are also clear that some people will fall away from God and return to a worldly lifestyle. Some will become apostates, from which there is no return.

It's important to understand that prayers are answered *because* we have fellowship with God! Luke 13:25; Matt. 25:12; 1 Tim. 4:1; 2 Thess. 2:3; 2 Pet. 2:20-22; Heb. 6:4-8; John 14:13-15; John 14:20-21, 23-24; John 15:7.

PRAYER

Father God,

Forgive me for breaking fellowship with You. Forgive me for trying to avoid conviction, and also allowing the busyness of life to cause me to neglect our relationship. I apologize, Holy Spirit, for grieving You and not giving You your rightful place in my life. Help me to come back into a relationship with You. I want to hear Your voice and have fellowship with You. Fill me with praise, worship, and prayer. Renew the right spirit in me. In Jesus's name, amen.

SPOUSES THAT DISRESPECT AND DISHONOR ONE ANOTHER

Scripture is clear that things such as treating spouses with disrespect, dishonor, and retaining offense have a lot to do with prayers being hindered. When there is discord and disunity in the family, it will definitely impact a couple's ability to receive answered prayer. It can also hinder people from being able to enter into a new season, open doors related to your destiny, ministry opportunities, and so much more. Spouses may not stop to think of those things as possible reasons why their prayers seem to be hindered. It can even affect the ability to prosper financially.

Prayers can be hindered due to strife, dishonor, and disrespect in marriage and family, and when a husband shows a lack of honor towards his wife. 1 Pet. 3:7.

Prayers are hindered by discord. Husbands, in a similar way, live with your wives with understanding since they are weaker than you are. Honor your wives as those who share God's life-giving kindness so that nothing will interfere {1465 Egkoptó } with your prayers. (1 Peter 3:7). That word in the Greek "Egkopto" means cut into (like blocking off a road); hinder by "introducing an obstacle that stands sharply in the way of a moving object" (Souter); (figuratively) sharply impede, by cutting off what is desired or needed; to block (hinder).[2]

When one or both spouses are not submitted to God or one another properly. Eph. 5:22-33.

---

[2] "Egkopto," Strong's Concordance #1465, https://biblehub.com/greek/1465.htm

When we step out of love and engage in evil speaking (1 Pet. 3:10-12).

Answers to prayer are received because we obey his commandments and do what pleases him (1 John 3:21-22).

The following prayer is a prayer to heal and restore marriages. Invite the Holy Spirit into your marriage.

PRAYER

Dear Heavenly Father,

We come together now asking that you forgive us for any areas where we have grieved Your Holy Spirit and not honored Your authority over our marriage. We make a covenant with Holy Spirit now, and we invite You to be the threefold cord between us that binds us together.

We ask that You, O God, be the shield round about us and our family. Help us to remember to ask for Your help. Come and refresh our marriage. You can make all things new. You can resolve issues that, on our own strength, we cannot. Breathe a fresh wind into us individually, but also into us as a couple. Renew our passion and desire for one another. Refresh what has become stale. Renew our friendship with one another. Give us eyes to see the best in one another.

Lord, heal us from our harshness and prejudices. Heal us from self-righteous convictions that are not from you. Help us to let go of pride, judgments, and other negative attitudes that make it difficult for us to truly love, understand, forgive and accept one another. Open our eyes to see each other with compassion and an understanding heart. Help us to walk in humility, confessing our sins to one another so that we may be healed, and our relationship can be restored.

Help us to understand what motivates one another without responding out of judgment or criticism. Help us to cover one another in love and to yield to one another without resentment. Fill us with Yourself, Holy Spirit. We need You.

We cannot revive ourselves. Please, help us come back into divine order in all things and shut the enemy out of our thoughts, our responses, our family, and our future. Help us shut the enemy out of our marriage and family.

We repent for anger, power struggles, poor communication, and any ways that we may have dishonored one another. We repent for any ways that we have rejected or disrespected one another. We choose to forgive each other for the past, and we resolve not to bring up old issues. We choose to place every old hurt, betrayal, and offense under the blood of Jesus.

We repent for any sins of ourselves or others in our family line that opened the door to adultery, jealousy, broken vows, and betrayal of trust or broken commitments.

Let the Blood of Jesus cover those sins. We believe You can heal our marriage and make it healthy. Let this be a brand-new day.

We renounce spirits known as Past, Regret, Fear, Jealousy, Unloving, Cold Love, Anger, Control, Condemnation, Disappointment, Disapproval, and Criticism. We repent for and renounce any ways we have entertained fault-finding that has made room for a spirit of Abuse in our conversations or actions.

We renounce any spirits that have come into our lives as a result of generational sin or disobedience on our part. We renounce the spirit known as Lilith, which ties us to Lust, Incubus, and Succubus spirits; all soul ties to former lovers, spouses, ungodly authority figures, and those that have sinned against us through abuse or sexual molestation.

We command all soul ties to go back to those individuals to whom they belong, and we ask that You, O God, restore our souls and make us whole, for Your word tells us in Psalm 23:3 that You restore our soul, and in Isaiah 53:5 Your word declares that 'by His stripes, we were healed."

We ask for a release of Your love and grace to help bring lasting change in our lives and marriage. In Jesus's Name, amen.

NOT SUBMITTED TO AUTHORITY

What we think matters just as much as how we relate to authority. A person can be compliant in their actions without actually being submitted in their heart. We are to be rightly subjected to the authority in our lives - husbands and wives, one to another, children to their parents. We are to be subject to the authority in our workplace and in the land where we live. We're to be subject to the laws of the land as much as possible. If we're out of order in any of those places, then are we truly submitted to the authority God has placed in our lives?

In order to effectively use the authority God gave you, you have to 1) know the law (His word) and, 2) you have to understand what it means to be under authority. Jesus commended the Roman Centurion in Matthew 8:5-13 for two qualities: Faith and submission. This centurion's servant was lying at home, paralyzed and suffering, so he came to ask Jesus to heal him. Jesus asked if he would like Him to come to his home, but the Roman centurion said, 'Oh, no, You don't need to come. Just send the word. I, too, am a man under authority. I tell my men, 'Do this, and they do it, or go there, and they go.' Jesus commended this man for understanding how authority works, and he marveled at his faith. He said, "Let it be done for you just as you thought it would."

Improper relationship to authority has consequences, esp. disrespecting authority, mocking or despising spiritual leaders. 2 Kings 2:23; Ps. 105:14-15; Gen. 20:7; Heb. 13:17; Luke 6:37; 1 Sam. 26:23; Acts 23:1-5. Additional scriptures: Eph. 4:2-3, Malachi 2:14-15, 1 Peter 3:7, Eph. 5:33, James 4:6,7.

PRAYER

Heavenly Father,

On behalf of myself and my ancestors, I ask Your forgiveness for rebellion to authority. Father, I haven't always felt that some people should be in authority, and I haven't respected them. I haven't had Your perspective towards authority, and in some cases, it's been difficult to honor certain people in positions of leadership. I haven't always honored You, or shown respect to my (husband/wife) and others in authority. I realize now it's about honoring their position rather than always agreeing with their decisions and conduct, but that is no excuse for speaking negatively about people.

Forgive me for speaking the wrong things about others. Let my speech be full of grace and edification for those that hear my words. Let my mouth be filled with wisdom. In Jesus's name, amen.

IGNORING THE POOR

Those who shut their ears to the cries of the poor will be ignored in their own time of need. Proverbs 21:13; Prov. 28:27.

The amount you give determines what you get back. Luke 6:38.

Guilty of withholding compassion, 1 John 3:17.

PRAYER

Heavenly Father,

Forgive me for turning a blind eye towards those in need. Forgive me for making judgments against people when I don't know their story. Lord, you have not called me to judge, but to love. Forgive me for stinginess and withholding help when it has been within my power to make a difference in the life of someone else. I'm sorry that I have not shown compassion towards the less fortunate more consistently, and more frequently. If I was hurting, I would want someone to help me, not judge or criticize me, or look down on me. Help me to have Your heart towards the less fortunate. Impress on my heart when and where you want me to bless someone, and also help me not talk myself out of being obedient to the leading of Your Spirit. In Jesus's name, amen.

MURMURING AND COMPLAINING

When God's people complained in the wilderness, He released thousands of snakes to bite them, and they died. Murmuring and complaining is a sign of an ungrateful heart, and that will keep people stuck. It is also referred to as testing God. Ref. 1 Corinthians 10:9-11.

Murmuring and complaining are equated with walking in a spirit of Lust, Jude 1:16.

It causes discontent and can cause the Lord to become angry. Numbers 11:4-10; Ex. 16:7-10.

Is considered rebellion towards the Lord. Deut. 1:26,27; Ps. 106:24-27.

Releases destruction. Jer. 9:12-17.

PRAYER

Heavenly Father,

Please forgive me for murmuring, complaining, and the wrong use of my words. I haven't always been good about bridling my tongue. Forgive me for rebellion, ingratitude, and testing You. I apologize for my lack of humility and for causing you to feel angry or upset with me.

I ask Your forgiveness for sowing discord or for allowing strife to come in because of my carelessness. Deliver my tongue from speaking unwholesome words, and please let the blood of Jesus cleanse me from all unrighteousness. In Jesus's name, amen.

INVOLVEMENT WITH THE OCCULT

Involvement with any form of witchcraft, fortunetelling, divination, or any form of occult practices is forbidden in scripture. It defiles those that have this spirit in their lives, cuts off relationships and communication with the Lord, and is a spiritual block to prayer. Deut. 18:9-14; Lev. 19:31; Lev. 20:6; 2 Kings. 17:14-15;1 Chron. 10:13-14; Rev. 21:8.

The presence of familiar spirits from occult involvement produces a great deal of bitterness, frustration, and setbacks in the lives of those that are affected. There is usually a sense of anxiety and fear also, because the presence of the enemy always comes with fear. The person may wrestle with feelings of anger, resentment, or a tendency to feel they are battling with God. The person feels they cannot seem to make any spiritual progress, but they don't know why. This wrestling causes them to feel as though God is unfair, when the reality is actually the opposite. It's the enemy that is making life so difficult.

Curses can take many forms, from being accident-prone, to financial problems, addictions to drugs and alcohol, lust, pornography, or addictions to masturbation, infertility, unable to find a marriage partner, and repeated cycles of broken relationships. Some people never break the cycle because they can't figure out what the problem is, but the symptoms indicate there is a spiritual root that must be dealt with in order to bring it to an end. Prayers will be frustrated until the cycle is completely broken.

PRAYER

Dear Heavenly Father,

I renounce and repent for any involvement with occult practices, secret societies, and the ungodly covenants they demand. (If you know which ones are involved in your family history, name them). I renounce and forsake all pledges, oaths, and agreements, as well as involvement with lodges, societies, or cults by my ancestors and myself.

I renounce and forsake all false gods, false doctrines, unholy communion, and abominations. I renounce and forsake the Luciferian doctrine. I renounce and forsake the oaths spoken to pledge loyalties to man or idol that violated the commands of God and conscience. I renounce all false masters associated with Freemasons, Shriners, Mormonism, Paganism, the Klu Klux Klan, the Illuminati, false religions, and their teaching. I renounce and forsake the false god Allah.

I renounce all occult activity, including channeling spirits, invoking the names of demonic spirits, praying to false gods and saints, and practicing pagan religious rituals and traditions. I renounce the works of darkness and want no benefit from it. I cancel any spiritual or natural inheritances that are forbidden by my Heavenly Father. I repent and renounce hypocrisy, the sins of mocking and scorning God, and all evil practices.

Father, I repent for making a covenant with Satan and any evil organizations where Satan is worshiped. I ask Your forgiveness for rebelling against You. I renounce any ceremonies that put me in a covenant with Satan and other demons. I renounce and forsake all words, phrases, and gestures used as secret codes. I break agreement with all curses that were once agreed to be placed upon any and all family members, including myself and future generations.

I renounce all familiar spirits assigned to my life and tell them in the name and authority of the Lord Jesus Christ to go back to hell, where they belong. I repent for blood ceremonies, human and animal sacrifice, and all abominable rituals and practices that I have participated in. I renounce all false spiritual fathers and mothers, mentors, and demonic guardians. I renounce all ceremonial indoctrination rituals that involve me or my ancestors, and I remove my family name from every evil altar. I come out of agreement with these covenants and evil spirits, and command them to leave me now in the name and authority of Jesus Christ. Let every curse associated with these abominations be broken now in Jesus's name.

I declare Jesus Christ is King of kings and Lord of lords, my Master, and my Savior. He is the risen Son of God, who died on my behalf and rose again victorious after defeating all the power of the enemy. I pledge myself to Jesus Christ all the days of my life. Holy Spirit, fill me with Your Spirit and lead me in the ways of truth and righteousness, in Jesus's name, amen.

ABORTION & SINS OF BLOODSHED

Abortion is the sin of premeditated murder towards the most innocent lives. Many people do not stop to consider that partaking in these crimes against humanity opens the door for a curse. The person that assists someone else in committing this sin is just as guilty, because they took part in helping bring the life of an innocent child to an end. There is guilt through association that causes people to have the stain of sin upon them (1 Tim. 5:22.; Rev. 18:4; Eph. 5:11).

Murder is a sin that will block answers to prayer (ref. Is. 1:15; Is. 59:2,3).

Murder releases a corresponding judgment (Matt. 5:21; Prov. 28:17).

Murder is a crime punished by death (Gen. 9:5,6; Ps. 9:12; 1 Kings 2:32).

Murder begins in the heart and is just as lethal if acted upon to physically take a life, as in slander and character assassination. It can block physical healing until repentance takes place. Jealousy, envy, contempt, rage, vengeance, retaliation, and covetous are intertwined with the spirit of murder (Deut. 32:35; Rom. 12:19; Matt. 23:31; Mark 7:21).

Murder releases a generational curse of premature death in the family line (2 Sam. 12:9-10).

Hatred is equated with murder and is evidence the person does not have eternal life (1 John 3:15).

Wandering, instability and the life of a vagabond is a curse for murder (Gen. 4:12-15).

The sin of bloodshed cries out to heaven to be avenged (Gen. 4:10; Rev. 6:10).

Bloodshed releases a curse on the land (Numbers 35:33; Ezek. 22:3-4; Ps. 106:38).

Murder excludes the unrepentant sinner from heaven (Gal. 5:21; Rev. 22:15).

God's mercy is available to all people. Saul, before his conversion to the Apostle Paul, killed many Christians thinking he was doing God's work but he was gravely mistaken. Upon his repentance, Saul was changed into a new man and went on to become a historical figure of great importance to the spread of the gospel. Confession of sin wipes out the stain of sin and shame, and the penalties of those sins are atoned for; this is why we place the blood of Jesus upon our sins and the iniquities in our bloodline. The blood of Jesus closes the door to the enemy so that he can no longer use those sins against us.

PRAYER

Father God,

I repent for the sins of premeditated murder and shedding innocent blood. I repent for any part I have played in participating, directly or indirectly, in taking the life of another human being.

I repent for taking away the justice of another person by ending their life. Forgive me for hard-heartedness, hatred, indifference, and playing god, taking justice and judgment into my own hands.

I repent for having hatred in my heart, evil speaking, slander, and character assassination. I repent for allowing jealousy, envy, contempt, rage, vengeance, covetousness, and a desire for revenge to be in my heart. I ask Your forgiveness for wanting _____ (be specific and name individuals) to suffer. Help me to let go of my anger and offense. Deliver me from wickedness and pull out the root of bitterness that's been in my heart.

Lord God, I cannot undo what I have done, but I pray for Your mercy and forgiveness. I ask that you tell (the person/people whose life you took) that I am truly sorry, and I ask for their forgiveness as well as Yours. I ask that the blood of Jesus would cover my sins and that You would show me mercy. I know I do not deserve it, but I thank You that You are gracious and forgiving. Help me to forgive myself for the wrongs that I have committed. Help me to know how to make amends to those I have hurt. Please cleanse my conscience of guilt, shame, and condemnation. Please let every curse of wandering, premature death, and punishment be canceled. I choose to serve You, Lord Jesus. Take my life and turn it into a testimony for Your glory. In Jesus's name, amen.

WISDOM TO DEFEAT THE ENEMY

CHAPTER THREE
VOWS, COVENANTS AND AGREEMENTS

The Bible teaches us that vows and covenants have great significance, both in the earthly realm as well as in the spiritual realm. A vow is a solemn pledge of a personal commitment either to another person, a deity or a saint. A covenant is a **commitment to fulfill** a vow or pledge, to make good on the promise. 'The term "covenant" is of Latin origin (con venire), meaning a coming together. It presupposes two or more parties who come together to make a contract, agreeing on promises, stipulations, privileges, and responsibilities.'[3]

A covenant is a bond between two parties, but it is also considered a treaty of sorts. Marriage is a covenant bond, and friendships or even business relationships can be considered covenant relationships as well. In many cases, such as a marriage or a business relationship, legal contracts must be executed, stipulating the terms that bring the relationship to an end. Many people today don't hold vows or covenants in high regard and break them without giving them much thought, but vows and covenants are legally binding in the spirit realm. Because they are legally binding, these agreements, vows, and covenants also require following spiritual protocols to ensure they are no longer enforceable.

Jesus cautions us to be careful about making vows and commitments for precisely that reason. In Matthew 5:33-37 it is written, "Again, you have heard that it was said to the people long ago, 'Do not break your oath, but keep the oaths you have made to the Lord.' But I tell you, Do not swear at all: either by heaven, for it is God's throne; or by the earth, for it is his footstool; or by Jerusalem, for it is the city of the Great King. And do not swear by your head, for you cannot make even one hair white or black. Simply let your 'Yes' be 'Yes,' and your 'No.' 'No'; anything beyond this comes from the evil one." He isn't referring to every vow, as in making a commitment to marriage. God honors covenant relationships. What He is saying is not to make a rash vow that will end up entrapping you in an unwise decision.

Prov. 20:25   "It is a trap to dedicate something rashly and only later to consider one's vows."

Vows can be made in a moment of personal pain or disappointment, such as, "I will never let anyone hurt me like that again," or "I will never trust anyone again." The person that does this makes an agreement to

---

[3] "Covenant," https://www.biblestudytools.com/dictionary/covenant/

construct invisible barriers of self-preservation in their heart because it's an attempt to guard themselves against being hurt and disappointed. It's actually a form of isolation because it prevents intimacy in relationships. However, that agreement remains legally binding in the spirit realm long after it's been forgotten. The day may come when the individual is ready for a new relationship (or realizes there is a serious underlying issue in their current relationship), but has difficulty trusting and developing intimacy with others. This is because the previously made vow is still on record, and the enemy has legal grounds to enforce it.

The individual gave away their legal rights to the enemy in a moment of pain when they spoke a rash vow, never stopping to consider how it might affect their future relationships. The reality is they ended up placing their already wounded heart into the hands of the enemy. Although the person never stopped to consider this, they set themselves up to be the god of their own heart, and that is called idolatry. All idolatry is rebellion against God, regardless of a person's intentions, and all idolatry comes with penalties for disobedience. Those 'invisible walls' that were intended to keep themselves from getting hurt also block a person's ability to develop intimacy with God. Walls keep everything out and keep the person trapped inside their own prison. In as much as we allow or disallow others to get close to us is the same degree to which we allow or disallow God to get close to us. It may not seem like it, but it's true.

God inhabits human vessels. That is who He has chosen to work through to complete His work on earth. If we cannot learn to trust others or hear spiritual truth from His messengers, the pride of our own hearts will end up deceiving us, and we will become prisoners within the confines of our own fortified walls. If the individual truly wants a breakthrough, they must verbally renounce the vow and let the enemy know it's been made void through repentance and the blood of Jesus. We must give Holy Spirit permission to blow up the lies that have kept the walls of our personal prisons in place, but it comes by freedom of choice. We are the only ones that can choose to take the walls down. Inner healing and deliverance can come no other way.

None of us know what the future holds or even if we are able to keep a vow, so it's best not to make a vow if you are not sure you can keep it. Sometimes we do end up saying something foolish or making a commitment to something too quickly without thinking it through, but God is merciful when we make mistakes. His counsel to us is not to make a promise to something if we are unsure of our ability to follow through with it, but all we need to do is confess our mistake and bring it under the blood of Jesus. "If we confess our sin, He is faithful and just and will forgive our sins and cleanse us from all unrighteousness."

1 John 1:9. Of course, if we have hurt someone in the process, then it is always important to make the situation right to the best of our ability.

We've addressed vows and covenants, but now let's look at the word 'agreement.' The word **agree** comes from **sumphoneo,** meaning "to be of the same mind," or "to come to a mutual understanding."[4] It means to be of one voice, in the same opinion or to form a mutual agreement. Matthew 18:18-20 teaches us the principle of agreement. When any two on earth agree in prayer, whatever they ask for will be done by their heavenly father. The power of agreement in the positive sense brings the Lord Jesus right into the midst of those praying in His name, and He promises that when there is such unity in prayer, what is requested will be granted.

The same principle of agreement also works in a negative sense, as in the case of Ananais and Saphira (ref. Acts 5). They were in mutual agreement but for the sake of deceiving others, which also incurred the execution of immediate divine judgment. Through these examples, we learn the importance of spiritual agreements. The enemy knows this, too. If we make an agreement with things that are aligned with anything found in the kingdom of darkness, such as distrust, unbelief, anger, bitterness or other things, then the enemy has legal grounds to take action, formulating his plan to bring those things to pass that we have agreed upon.

We might not have understood we were placing our agreement with him, but anything that is not aligned with faith is fair game. One of the most sobering truths of the Bible is the latter part of Romans 14:23, where the Apostle Paul makes the statement that "whatever is not of faith is sin," because at the root of every single issue of our lives is a reality check. Either we trust God, or we don't. We are either aligned with faith or we are not, and if we are not, then we are guilty of sin. Regardless of how we may tend to justify our fears, insecurities, doubts and double-mindedness, or the many ways we may attempt to justify our excuses, the spiritual realm is based on cold, hard truth.

Sin is not defined by our thoughts, feelings, or a variety of opinions; sin is defined by its root. Where is the point of agreement? Is it faith or unbelief? Our confession and our actions testify to what we truly believe. Faith is the conviction that what we hope for, the thing we pray for, does indeed exist, it is obtainable, and we can call it into our present reality. We must learn not to lean on our own understanding but, in all our ways, acknowledge God. We must know His word and line up our confession to scripture so that we deny spirits of darkness anything they can use against us.

---

[4] "Symphonos," Strongs Concordance #4859, https://biblehub.com/greek/4859.htm

Of course, none of us adhere to the word perfectly. There is grace available when we miss the mark, and we don't have to live under condemnation, but if we truly want to live a victorious life in Christ, then our aim is to take back every bit of ground that we have given up through ignorance to God's word, areas of disobedience and compromise.

PRAYER

Father God,

Please remind me of any vows, agreements or covenants that I have made, and uncover those that my ancestors made, giving the enemy legal grounds to form an assignment against my family and me. (Listen for God to speak, to show you an image or bring up a past memory before you proceed.)

I repent for any vows, agreements or covenants that were made with Satan and his workers of darkness and evil. (Be specific in this next part wherever possible). I renounce the inner vow I made when I said, "_____." Forgive me for not trusting You with the safekeeping of "_____" (my heart, my family, my finances, my future, etc.). Forgive me for making myself god of my own life.

Forgive me for justifying wrong thoughts and beliefs that have blinded me to my own self-deception and caused me to align myself with unbelief. I confess this sin. I place all of me and the issues of my life in Your capable hands, Lord. I place the blood of Jesus upon any words that were spoken by myself or anyone else in my family line that made some sort of covenant or agreement with others that were unwise. I void all those contracts and declare they are unenforceable from this moment on. Thank You, Father, for healing my heart and healing my faith. In Jesus's name, amen.

There is another aspect to consider when it comes to the power of agreement, because, really, this is all about the power of our words.

Matt 12:36-37   "But I say to you that for every idle word men may speak, they will give an account of it in the day of judgment. For by your words you will be justified, and by your words you will be condemned."

Prov. 18:21   "The tongue can bring death or life; those who love to talk will reap the consequences."

The wrong use of our words can release the enemy on assignments. When we speak negatively about certain people or situations, we can actually give the enemy legal grounds to act upon the words we speak. This is true, especially in the lives of our loved ones because we have authority in our realm of influence. We have the creative power of God inside of us because we are made in His image. Let us be careful to guard our words and speak what is edifying, lest we give the enemy his next assignment!

PRAYER

Father God,

I come before You and I confess that my words in regard to my loved ones have not always been full of faith. At times, in my frustration, I have been careless and spoken things that have not been positive. I ask Your forgiveness for speaking negative words over my family members and giving Satan legal grounds to act upon those words.

I repent for every negative confession that hangs over my loved ones as a curse waiting to come to pass. I condemn the power of those words, and I declare that those words will no longer resound in the airwaves. I cancel every word cursed over me and my family. I put the blood of Jesus on those negative words, and I declare they will not come to pass in Jesus's name. That agreement in the spiritual realm is broken now in Jesus's name, and from this moment on, it is unenforceable.

I bless my family members. (List them by name. Speak blessing over them individually).

I declare they will fulfill their destiny in Christ, and they will bring you great pleasure, Father. I declare my children will fulfill the will of God for their lives. I bind the spirit of rebellion, resentment, and lawlessness in Jesus's name. I bind the works of evil in their lives and forbid all evil assignments from coming to pass in Jesus's name. I release the Spirit of Repentance, Humility, and the conviction of the Holy Spirit to draw them to repentance and position them in right alignment with the Lord. I declare my loved ones are born again, set free and delivered from all that has had them bound in Jesus's name. I declare they are full of peace and joy. They are delivered from negative mindsets, rejection, guilt, condemnation and shame. I declare we are all quick to forgive and extend love and grace to others. I declare my loved ones are not slaves to any form of bondage.

They are children of the Most High God, and they walk in truth, integrity, love and liberty. My loved ones, including my (husband/wife) and I, are committed to walking with the living God all the days of our lives, and we will not fall away. Our love will not grow cold in Jesus's name. Our hearts burn with conviction towards what is good and right in Your eyes, and we turn away from those things you call evil. I thank you that our minds are free from confusion, temptation and double-mindedness. Our hearts are full of faith in You, and I declare we are blessed and highly favored by the Lord. Our health is blessed. Our home and finances are blessed. We are blessed coming in, and we are blessed going out. The blessings are chasing us down and being put in our hands. I declare we are a blessing to many others, in Jesus's name, amen.

DECLARATIONS OF FAITH OVER FAMILY AND CHILDREN

I exalt You as the Name above every other name that has attempted to release oppression over my life and the lives of my children.

I exalt You as LORD over every circumstance. I thank You that YOU are exalted over (insert name) _____'s life.

I praise You for the way You lead (_____) by the hand and help (him/her) navigate through tight places.

I praise You for the way You restore our hope and help us overcome discouraging thoughts.

I thank You and praise You for teaching (_____) Your ways, so that his/her soul can prosper and he/she can be in health.

I thank You for getting his/her mind off of unfruitful thoughts so that he/she can see your beauty.

I thank You, Holy Spirit, for sifting out the things that don't even need to be in my prayers.

I thank You, Holy Spirit, for showing me how to pray in such a way as to glorify Christ instead of my fears, concerns or circumstances.

I praise You for the way You work through the impossibilities of (_____'s) life.

I praise You that You are in control.

I praise You that You watch over Your word to bring it to pass.

I praise You because I know that my prayers have been heard and I have what I have requested.

I praise You for the things I can see working in (_____'s) life and the things I don't see.

I praise You for the way that You are able to take every circumstance and redeem it to bring hope and something that works for her good.

I praise You that You are the One who knows how to bring the missing pieces together.

I praise You for being the One who loves (_____) and aligns (_____) for blessing.

I praise You that You are the One who leads him/her into the good plans You have for him/her.

I praise You for showing (_____) his/her true identity in Christ, and that the Spirit of Adoption is released into their life to reveal to him that he is Your son/daughter.

I praise You for helping (_____) cut off all worldly affections in his/her life and for turning his/her heart towards You.

I praise You for (_____'s) salvation and deliverance that is taking place now.

I thank You and praise You that (_____) is fully committed to living for You.

I thank You and praise You that (_____) has surrendered his/her life to You. I thank You for making surrender easy for him/her.

I thank You and praise You for releasing the Spirit of Truth into my son's/daughter's life and exposing the lies of the enemy.

I thank You and praise You for revealing the Fatherhood of God to (_____).

I thank You for revealing to (_____) the love of God, Your acceptance and the delight You take in him/her because he/she is Yours.

I thank You that (_____) will praise You for himself/herself and realize that You have good plans for him/her according to Jeremiah 29:11.

I thank You that You have become (_____'s) compass, drawing him/her to Yourself.

I praise You for my breath. I thank You for breathing life into my child.

I praise You for his/her life, the gifts You've given him/her and that he/she will use them for Your glory.

I thank You for drawing my children to Your heart and revealing Jesus to them.

I thank You that when I praise You, I see You in the highest place, and my problems come into perspective.

I thank You that when I praise You, my faith is lifted, and I get a spiritual upgrade.

I thank You that when I praise you, prison doors are opened, and I am released from captivity.

I thank You that when I praise You, the invisible barriers are broken.

I thank You that when I praise You, I receive revelation and inspired thoughts from You.

I thank You that You are the answer to everything I need and everything my son/daughter needs. I thank You that You are faithful to answer my prayers because You love him/her even more than I do.

I thank You that You are able to get through to those that I cannot reach.

I thank You that when I praise You, the heavy yoke falls off.

I thank You that when I praise You, my perception of Your greatness explodes in my heart.

I thank You that when I praise You, my expectancy towards You increases.

I thank You that when I praise you, I know that nothing is impossible with You. Amen.

CHAPTER FOUR
STRONGHOLDS AND STRONGMEN

A stronghold is defined as 1) a fortified place, 2) a place of security or survival, or 3) a place marked by a particular group or by a particular characteristic.[5] The Longman's Dictionary of military terms also defines it as a place where there is a lot of support or an area that is strongly defended by a military group.[6] In a spiritual sense, the strongholds that we face are lies in our belief system that cause us to become self-deceived or blinded to truth in some area of our thinking.

One common stronghold people wrestle with is unforgiveness. A person can intellectually agree with scripture that it is good and necessary to forgive others, yet still, have a great deal of difficulty getting their heart to agree and submit to the authority of God. Judgments that they have made over another individual help them justify their lack of forgiveness. Although they can speak the words that they have forgiven a person that offended them, their heart may not be as willing. This is one example of a stronghold.

Strongholds are often tied to an area of sin in a person's life, and secrecy keeps the person bound to that particular sin. Sin and shame need secrecy to stay alive. Sin can only thrive in darkness and isolation. When a person tries to avoid conviction of the Holy Spirit, they partner with self-deception. Self-deception will lie to a person and help them justify their sin, telling them that it's not really that bad until the person has lost sensitivity to the Holy Spirit and no longer believes their wrongdoing is a sin. It could be a same-sex relationship, an addiction, gossip, lying or something else that becomes a habitual sin.

The best way to identify whether or not a person has a stronghold working in their life is to ask God. This is an exercise that would benefit from writing down what you hear in prayer.

1. Pray: Father, is there a stronghold in my thinking that You want to reveal to me?

2. Will You show me a scripture that speaks on this issue?

3. Ask God: When did I first open the door to this sin? What was going on in my life?

---

[5] "Stronghold," Merriam-Webster Online Dictionary, https://www.merriam-webster.com/dictionary/stronghold
[6] "Stronghold," Longman's Dictionary of Contemporary English, https://www.ldoceonline.com/Military-topic/stronghold

4. What personal benefit do I receive from participating in this habit/sin? What am I trying to avoid? What am I trying to satisfy through illegitimate means?

5. Ask yourself: Do I want to remain in self-deception, giving the enemy legal grounds to rob me, or do I want to be a person of integrity, walking in truth and righteousness?

6. Holy Spirit, what is the truth You want to show me? I give You permission to convict me of sin and righteousness.

7. Pray: Father, I acknowledge my sin and ask You to give me the power to break the strongholds in my life. I renounce the lies I have believed and the spiritual agreements that have been made with the enemy. I break those agreements and declare from this day forth they are unenforceable. I place the blood of Jesus upon them and cancel those assignments in Jesus's name.

8. Pray: Father, what do You want to give me to replace this habit/behavior/void in my life?

9. Pray: Father, I ask for You to help me see the way of escape so that I do not run back to this sin and help me not to justify this area of weakness anymore.

10. Holy Spirit, I give you permission to give me pure desires and to lead me away from temptation, in Jesus's name, amen.

Strongholds can take up many areas of a person's thinking, and actions are born out of each individual's belief system. For instance, a person that feels as though their parents favored a sibling over them might grow up with the lies that they are inferior, and a stronghold of jealousy, insecurity, or rejection might be a very strong influence in that person's life. Another person may have grown up in poverty and later becomes a workaholic in order to try to alleviate the fear of financial lack. These are two examples of strongholds at work in people's lives. A network of lies is reinforced to keep the stronghold in place.

This is a defense mechanism to maintain a false belief system so that the individual does not surrender that place in their heart to the Lord. When a person does not trust God with an area of their life, they create habits and behaviors that they control and allow the enemy to lord over. It becomes a works-based, performance-oriented system of acceptance and approval. Sometimes this is in reference to obtaining God's approval, our own approval or the approval of others. There will also be a lack of intimacy with God when strongholds exist. Strongman spirits rule over various areas of a person's thought life, keeping them under the control and influence of that particular spirit.

Luke 11:21-22   "When a strong man, fully armed, guards his own house, his possessions are safe. But when someone stronger attacks and overpowers him, he takes away the armor in which the man trusted and divides up his plunder." NIV

Jesus instructed us to 'bind the strongman' before we could plunder his house and take away the spoils. The strongman is Satan, and the armor that he trusts in are the lies, arguments and twisted thinking that are formulated by his underlying demons. It is the power of evil that keeps Satan's dominion in place. In scripture, houses represent a person or a family. The house of the strongman is the person that is oppressed. Obviously, the person stronger than the enemy is the Lord, and He is the One that ultimately 'binds the strongman' through the prayers of God's people. Because the stronghold is based on lies and deception, the only thing that will set the person free is for them to recognize where they have embraced a lie. A soul that is oppressed by a strongman spirit is blind to the truth and often has no desire to pray for their own freedom.

2 Cor. 4:4   "Satan, who is the God of this world, has blinded the minds of those who don't believe. They are unable to see the glorious light of the Good News. They don't understand this message about the glory of Christ, who is the exact likeness of God." NLT

This encompasses all who are bound by unbelief in some area of their belief system. They are blind to something that God considers sin in their life. On a side note: God will communicate in other ways to get their attention, often in dreams. Sometimes, this shows up in a person's dreams as a squid or an octopus spirit. The octopus or squid represents an influence that has made the person 'spineless,' 'timid,' or spiritually weak in confronting and addressing a particular issue. The tentacles or arms of the squid and octopus represent the multiple spirits working together or the multiplied strength of the spirits keeping the individual blind to their need for deliverance.

The spiritual strongman is described as being 'fully armed,' meaning he is ready to do battle to protect his stronghold. When we are dealing with a strongman spirit, it is important to 'bind the strongman' before we attempt to recover the spoils (souls) or we will simply enrage him and cause him to further strengthen his grip on the captive(s). Arguments and defenses are raised to fortify itself against the truth of God's word. Because it is demonically energized and strengthened, it can feel impossible to break the power of the enemy's grip, but all things ARE possible in Christ. Natural reasoning is not powerful enough to break the power of the enemy's lie; only the word of God is anointed to demolish the lies and arguments that resist the truth. Jesus IS synonymous with the word of God, and the word of God is powerful and effective in destroying strongholds. We are advised in Ephesians 6:14-17 to put on our spiritual armor so that we are prepared for battle. We take up the sword of the Spirit and our shield of faith to quench the fiery darts and extinguish every lie.

2 Cor.10:5   "We destroy arguments and every lofty opinion raised against the knowledge of God, and take every thought captive to obey Christ … ."

Binding the strongman renders the strongman spirit powerless, at least temporarily, which gives the Holy Spirit the opportunity to release truth and revelation that will set the captive free. Bind the name of the strongman and then lose the counterpart of the Holy Spirit and the gifts of the Holy Spirit. It may not happen the first time, or the second time, or even the third, but persistence in prayer will eventually shift a situation, because "You are of God little children and have overcome them because greater is He that is in you than he that is in the world" (1 John 4:4).

Who have we overcome? The Antichrist spirits in the world. The lying spirits that oppose the word of God. If we continue to exercise our faith in prayer, we will prevail! There are some very obvious signs of demonic oppression that include:

_ Nightmares, night terrors, sleep paralysis, or feeling touched in a sexual way during the night.

_ Feelings of heaviness, discouragement, depression and hopelessness.

_ Tendencies towards self-harm or suicidal thoughts.

_ Fear and anxiety or panic attacks.

_ Thoughts that trigger fear and anxiety, like PTSD that cause 'fight or flight' responses.

_ Scratches or symbols appearing in a person's flesh out of nowhere.

_ Inability to rest or sleep on a consistent basis.

_ Seeing dark shadows move in your home. Seeing actual demons or shadow figures.

_ The feeling of being watched by some invisible being.

_ Unexplained health issues, repeated sicknesses, and doctors' inability to find the root cause of illness.

_ Marriage or relationship failures.

_ Continued "bad luck" with accidents, repeated cycles of loss, breakdown of cars, etc.

_ Long-term financial problems. Generational poverty.

_ Anger, rage, problems with unforgiveness, desire for vengeance.

_ The feeling of being touched by some unseen presence.

_ Uncontrollable lust, masturbation or sexual sins, addiction to porn and unclean thoughts.

_ Hearing voices, the presence of familiar spirits or communicating with the dead.

_ Inability to feel at peace or rest in the presence of other believers or a church atmosphere.

_ Things moving by themselves in a home, flickering lights, unexplained noises, doors slamming.

_ Unexplained lack of control over various parts of your body, such as arms or legs moving.

_ Hating God, mocking God, and abusiveness towards others.

_ Drug and alcohol addiction or other addictions. (False forms of comfort or self-soothing.)

_ Deliberate disobedience, engaging in unbecoming conduct.

_ Rebellion to authority, challenging authority figures.

_ Pathological lying.

_ Narcissistic behavior.

_ Obsessive-compulsive behaviors, including being obsessed with other people.

_ Strong need to control or manipulate others.

_ Feeling oppressed by shame, guilt or condemnation, or using those emotions to control others.

_ Defiance, arguing, constant complaining.

_ Feeling satisfaction when inflicting intentional emotional wounding upon others.

_ Engages in self-pity, blame-shifting, has a victim mentality, refuses to take responsibility.

_ Participation in occult practices.

Demons are identified by their function. Examine the fruit and trace it back to the root. The following list of strongman spirits can be used as a guide or a diagnostic tool to help you identify particular demon groupings of, what they represent, and the characteristics of each spirit. It is also important to realize that these spirits often show up as emotions, thoughts or feelings but can also be demonic entities (with an assignment) by that same name. The strongman is like a general or a lieutenant in Satan's army. There are various ranks of demonic spirits underneath each strongman.

Strongman	Characteristics & Manifestations	Scripture References	Comments
Spirit of Divination Also known as the spirit of Python	Fortune-teller, False prophecy, Soothsayer, Warlock, Satanist, Witch, Wiccan, Pagan practices, Astrology and Horoscopes, Rebellion, Hypnotist, Ventriloquism, Enchanter, Waterwitching/Divination, Magic, Constriction, Feels like suffocation, Financial Constriction, Heart, Breathing and Back Problems	Acts 16:16-18; Micah 5:12; Isaiah 2:6; Exodus 22:18; Isaiah 47:13; Leviticus 19:26; Jeremiah 10:2; 1 Samuel 15:23; Deuteronomy 18:11; Isaiah 19:3; Galatians 5:20, Revelation 9:21; 18:23; 21:8; 22:15; Hosea 4:12; Exodus 7:11; 8:7; 9:11	Bind: the Spirit of Divination/Python Loose: The Holy Spirit and Gifts Bind: Spirit of Leviathan, Bitterness & Pride Loose: Humility, a Spirit of Repentance
Familiar Spirit	Necromancer, Medium, Peeping and Muttering, Yoga, Clairvoyant, Spiritist, Passive Mind Dreamers. Familiar spirits tend to run in families. Spirits that imitate deceased family members.	Deuteronomy 18:11; 1 Chronicles 10:13; 1 Samuel 28; Isaiah 8:19; 29:4; 59:3; Jeremiah 29:8; 1 Samuel 28:7,8; Galatians 5:20; Revelations 9:21; 18:23; 21:8; 22:15	Bind: Familiar Spirits Loose: Holy Spirit and Gifts of the Spirit,. Spirit of Truth & Revelation
Spirit of Jealousy	Murder Slander, Gossip, Revenge-Spite, Anger-Rage, Hatred, Cruelty, Strife, Contention, Competition, Covetousness, Envy, Cause Divisions, Desire for Superiority Over Others	Genesis 4:4-6; 37:3,4,8; Proverbs 6:34; 10:12; 13:10; 14:16-17,29-30; 22:24-25; 27:4; 29:22-23; Numbers 5:14,30; 1 Thessalonians 4:8; Song of Solomon 8:6; Galatians 5:19	Bind: Jealousy Loose: Love of God
Lying Spirit	Strong Deceptions, Flattery, Superstitions, Religious Bondages, False Prophecy, Accusations, Slander, Gossip, Lies, False Teachers	2 Chron. 18:22; Psalms 31:18; 78:36; Proverbs 6:16- 19; 10:18; 20:19; 26:28; 29:5; Jeremiah 23:16-17; Matt.7: 15	Bind: Lying Spirit Loose: Spirit of Truth
Perverse Spirit	Broken Spirit, Evil Actions, Atheist, Abortion, Child Abuse,	Exodus 20:13; 21:22-25; Proverbs 1:22; 2:12; 14:2; 15:4;	Bind: Perverse Spirit, Idolatry

	Filthy Mind, Doctrinal Error, Sex Perversions, Twisting the Word of God, Foolish, Chronic Worrier, Contentions, Incest, Pornography, Works in relationship to Lust, Masturbation, Incubus/Succubus spirits, Sexual addiction	17:20,23; 19:1,3; 23:33; Isaiah 19:14; Acts 13:10; Romans 1:17-32; Philippians 2:14-16; 1 Timothy 6:4,5; 2 Timothy 3:2,7-8; Titus 3:11,11; 2 Peter 2:14	Loose: God's Spirit; Purity, Holiness Spirit of Humility and Repentance, Spirit of Liberty
Spirit of Haughtiness	Arrogant-Smug, Pride, Anti-Christ, Scornful, Strife, Obstinate, Self-Deception, Contentious, Self-Righteous, Rebellion, Rejection of God	1 Samuel 15:23; 2 Samuel 22:8; Proverbs 1:22; 3:34; 6:16,17; 10:4; 13:10; 16:18,19; Luke 18:11,12	Bind: Haughtiness and pride, anti-Christ spirit Loose: Humble and Contrite Spirit
Spirit of Heaviness	Excessive Mourning, Sorrow-Grief, Insomnia, Self-Pity, Discouragement, Rejection, Broken-Heart, Despair, Dejection, Hopelessness, Depression, Suicide, Inner Hurts, Torn Spirit, Heaviness	Isaiah 61:3; Luke 4:18; Nehemiah 2:2; Proverbs 15:13; Psalms 69:20; Proverbs 12:18; 15:3,13; 18:14; Luke 4:18; 2 Corinthians 1:8-9; Isaiah 61:3; Mark 9; Luke 4:18; Proverbs 18:14; 26:22	Bind: Spirit of Heaviness Loose: Holy Spirit as Comforter, Garment of Praise, Oil of Joy
Spirit of Whoredom	Unfaithfulness, Adultery, Spirit-Soul-or-Body Prostitution, Chronic Dissatisfaction, Love of Money, Fornication, Lust, Idolatry, Selfish, Vanity, Worldliness, Ambition	Ezekiel 16:15,28; Proverbs 5:1-14; Galatians 5:19; Proverbs 15:27; 1 Timothy 6:7-14; Hosea 4:13-19	Bind: Spirit of Whoredom Loose: Spirit of God: Purity, Passion for His Presence
Spirit of Infirmity	Bent Body-Spine, Impotent, Frail, Lame, Asthma-Hay Fever-Allergies, Arthritis, Weakness, Lingering Disorders, Oppression, Cancer, Lingering Unexplained Illness and Disease; Breakdown of the Body.	Luke 13:11; John 5:5; Acts 3:2; 4:9; Acts 10:38	Bind: Spirit of Infirmity Loose: Spirit of Resurrection Life and Gifts of Healing.

Deaf and Dumb Spirit	Dumb-Mute, Crying, Drowning, Tearing, Blindness, Mental Illness, Ear Problems, Suicidal, Foaming At The Mouth, Seizures/ Epilepsy, Gnashing Of Teeth	Matt. 9:32,33; 12:22; 15:30-31; 17:15; Mark 5:5; 9:18,22,25-26,39 Luke 9:39	Bind: Deaf and Dumb Spirit Loose: Resurrection Life and Gifts of Healing
Spirit of Bondage	Fears, Addictions, Drugs, Alcohol, Cigarettes, Food, Masturbation and Sexual Sins, Fear of Death, Captivity to Satan, Servant of Corruption, Compulsive Sin, Bondage to Sin	Rom. 6:16; 7:23; 8:15; 2 Peter 2:19; Heb. 2:14-15; Luke 8:23; John 8:34; Acts 8:23; Proverbs 5:2; 2 Tim. 2:26	Bind: Spirit of Bondage Loose: Liberty, Spirit of Adoption
Spirit of Fear	Fears, Phobias, Heart Attacks, Torment-Horror, Fear of Man, Nightmares, Terrors, Anxiety-Stress, Fear of Death, Untrusting, Doubt, Perfectionism, Compulsions, Arrested Development, Stuck in Childhood	Isaiah 13:7-8; 2 Tim. 1:7; Psalms 55:4-5; 1 John 4:18; Luke 21:26; John 14:1,27; Prov. 29:25; Jer. 1:8; 17-19; Ezek. 2:6-7; 3:9; Psalms 91:5-6; Isaiah 54:14; Heb. 2:14-15; 1 Peter 5:7; Matt.8:26; Rev. 21:8	Bind: Spirit of Fear Loose: Love of God, Resurrection Power, Truth and Revelation
Seducing Spirits	Hypocritical Lies, Seared Conscience, Attractions, Fascinations by False Prophets, Signs and Wonders, Deception, Wandering from the Truth, Fascination with Evil Ways, Objects or Persons, Seducers, Enticers	1 Tim.4:1; Proverbs 12:22; James 1:14; Mark 13:22; Rom. 7:11; 2 Thes. 2:10; 2 Tim. 3:13; 1 John 2:18-26; Deut. 13:6-8; 2 Tim. 3:13; Prov. 1:10; 12:26; 2 Tim. 3:13	Bind: Seducing Spirits Loose: Holy Spirit of-Truth
Spirit of Anti-Christ	Denies Deity of Christ, Denies Atonement, Against Christ and His Teaching, Humanism, Worldly Speech and Actions, Teachers of Heresies, Anti-Christian, Deceiver, Lawlessness, Mocking, Scorning,	1 John 2:18,19; 1 John 4:3,5; 2 John 1:7; 2 Thes. 2:4,3-12; Rev. 13:7	Bind: Spirit of Anti-Christ, Pride, Rebellion Loose: Spirit of Truth, Humility, Repentance, Spirit of Adoption

	Dishonor, Disrespect towards God and His servants		
Spirit of Abandonment	Isolation, Victim Mentality Rejection, Loneliness, Feels Unwanted, Feels Unloved Like An Orphan, Inferiority, Insecurity, Anger, Resentment	Ps. 27:10-14; Heb. 13:5; Eph. 1:6	Bind: Spirit of Abandonment Loose: Spirit of Adoption
Leviathan	Stubborn, Lying, Hardheaded, Unrepentant, Debating, Insubordinate, Argumentative, Mocking, Scoffer, Twists Truth	Job 41:34	Bind: Spirit of Leviathan and Pride Loose: Humility, Grace of God, Spirit of Repentance
Spirit of Insanity/Mental Illness	Paranoia, Torment, Obsessive-Compulsive Confusion, Compulsions, Insanity, Schizophrenia, Hallucinations, Hysteria	Deut. 28:20-28, 2 Tim. 1:7	Bind: Spirit of Insanity/Mental Illness Loose: Spirit of Truth, Power of God, Love
Spirit of Death	Unexplained Terminal Health Issues, Untimely Death, Extreme Poverty, Generational Curse of Death in the Family	Prov. 18:21, Eph. 4:18, 1 John 5:12, Rev. 6:5,6, Deut. 28:20-28, Rom 6:16, Rom. 8:13	Bind: Spirit of Death and Hell Loose: Holy spirit/Spirit of Resurrection life, Gifts of Holy Spirit
Spirit of Apollyon/ Abaddon	Destruction, Destroyer Spirits, Unexplained Tendencies Towards Accidents and Near Death Experiences, Things That Devour and Destroy , Mental Torment	Rev. 9:11, Exodus 10:12-20; Joel 1:4, Ezekiel 2:6, Lk 11:12	Bind: Spirit of Apollyon Loose: Spirit of Repentance, Humility
Rejection	Feelings of Unworthiness, Withdraw from Others & Isolation, Self-Hatred, Anorexia, Bulimia, Cutting and Self-Harm, Looks for Acceptance, Addictions, Rejects Others. Physical Issues Develop Such as Auto Immune Diseases.	2 Kings 13:23, Rom. 11:1; John 6:37; Acts 10:34,35; Eph. 1:6	Bind: Rejection Loose: Spirit of Love and Acceptance, Spirit of Truth, Spirit of Adoption

Bitterness	Unforgiving, Resentment, Blaming, Anger, Slander and Evil Speaking, Sins of Murder with The Mouth and Character Assassination, Desire for Vengeance, Affects Physical Body With Digestive Disorders, Gall Bladder Issues	1 Sam. 18-19; Job 2:9; Acts 8:14-24; Eph. 4:31; Heb. 12:15; James 3:13-18.	Bind: Bitterness and Unforgiveness Loose: Spirit of Mercy and Forgiveness, Spirit of Repentance

BREAKING CYCLES OF ARRESTED DEVELOPMENT

People often wonder, where do deliverance ministers learn about all these different types of spirits? They don't see some of these things in scripture, but many times people are also not digging deeper to examine the truth that is in the word. Much of what I've learned has come from personal experience. Some of it has been from scripture, and other things have been a result of revelation from the Holy Spirit. The Bible is not a fully formed textbook. There are things we learn with experience and from the experience of others that allows us to grow and continue to learn. John 21:25 tells us that Jesus also did many more things that are not contained in the scriptures, so there will always be an opportunity to grow in the knowledge of spiritual matters if we are humble and teachable.

I would like to introduce you to another group of spirits that work together called 'Arrested Development.' Arrested Development is a psychological term that describes mental, emotional or physical impairment, but some deliverance ministers have reported dealing with a strongman type of demon that calls itself by that name. The spirit of Arrested Development can cause grown adults to revert to childlike behavior such as pouting and crying, stubbornness, anger, temper tantrums, and other things. It also halts their progress and keeps them trapped by a lack of emotional development.

I have dealt with many people that struggle with various disorders, and what I see most often are spiritually-rooted issues. There are many demons that are responsible for certain types of behaviors that manifest as mental health issues. There are many people, children included, that suffer from impairment issues for a variety of reasons. There was a man born blind in John chapter 9 and some of Jesus's disciples asked him, "Who sinned? This man or his parents?" Jesus said neither, but it was for the purpose of bringing glory to God. The reality is we live in a fallen world where there are influences around us that negatively affect people. Sometimes it is the result of spiritual oppression, and other times it is simply because, at some point, that person is destined to receive a healing that will bring glory to the Father. Either way, our approach should be to do what we know to do in confessing any known sin, thank God for healing, and allow God to do what He does best.

Demons look for areas where they have legal grounds or the cooperation of the individual's will in order to oppress them. They can either gain access through open doors in the family line, or they can gain cooperation by manipulating a person's belief system. When a person suffers from some sort of emotional wounding, demons exploit a person's pain and seize that moment to introduce their lies. That is why we are counseled by the word of God to offer our bodies – every part of us – to God as a living sacrifice and not allow ourselves to be conformed to the things in this world (ref. Rom. 12:1-2). This isn't just referring to outward behaviors but it also addresses our inner thought life. We are advised to 'renew our minds' so that we understand what the good and acceptable will of God is for us. The devil is an opportunist, always seeking whom he may devour.

1 Pet. 5:8,9   "Be sober, be vigilant because your adversary the devil walks about like a roaring lion, seeking whom he may devour. Resist him, steadfast in the faith, knowing that the same sufferings are experienced by your brotherhood in this world."

Demons look for ways to capitalize on situations where they can introduce the spirit of Fear. Fear is their number one weapon. From that entry point, the enemy can lead the person in a variety of directions. Fear, Rebellion, Confusion, Apollyon and the Deaf & Dumb spirit join forces to cause physical, mental and emotional problems. Therefore, it stands to reason that many things that are labeled mental health or psychological issues can have a root cause that is spiritual, not necessarily of physical origin.

Spiritually-rooted issues can only be solved by dealing with demonic spirit(s) responsible for the condition. However, psychologists and doctors are not deliverance ministers; therefore, they must find a way to treat their patients within the scope of their expertise and training. Please understand that I am not saying there cannot be legitimate medical reasons behind some of the conditions listed below, and I'm not saying that demons are responsible for every issue. However, in many cases, a patient cannot receive treatment or other forms of help *unless* they are diagnosed by a licensed medical practitioner. Medical practitioners are not going to diagnose spiritually-rooted issues. Demons also don't leave with medication or counseling.

When I was about 13, I went to a psychologist for depression. After meeting with this person one time for about an hour, he declared I would never mature emotionally. I shut down in his office because I was uncomfortable. That wasn't a psychological assessment; it was a critical judgment. This negative assessment hung over my life as a word curse for a long, long time. I remember crying all the way home and feeling the pain and resentment from this person's words, and the way that information was communicated to me. I was covered in shame and humiliation at the thought that I was somehow defective. The thought of never being able to be a fully functioning adult created a sense of embarrassment, insecurity, shame, and fear about the future. I went from being depressed to angry, rebellious, and feeling emotions that were completely out of control. The enemy used a mental health professional to inflict emotional injury. Nothing positive came from that encounter.

I am sure I am not the only person to experience the painful effect of being stamped with a negative label. **Words are powerful.** I went through many years of professional counseling for deep depression and was prescribed many medications, but I never got better from that course of treatment because the root of my issues was connected to sin and demonic oppression. I got better when I started dealing with sin and growing in my relationship with Christ. I believe a great deal that cannot be explained by health professionals gets falsely labeled in order to get treatment for the patient. In my own life I know this is true because I had a counselor tell me so. I could not get treatment or medication unless they could label me with a diagnosis found in their Diagnostic and Statistical Manual for Mental Disorders. I had many things out of order because I wasn't in the right relationship with God. Demons were trying to destroy me through mental torment.

Some of the issues and disorders connected to Arrested Development are:

- Oppositional Defiance Disorder

- Conduct Disorders

- Schizophrenia and other Delusional Disorders

- Anorexia, Bulimia and Eating Disorders

- Learning Disabilities, Mental Blocks and Confusion Disorders

- Children who don't want to grow up, Tantrums and Immaturity Disorders

- Stunted Emotional Growth, Self-sabotage, and Irresponsibility

- Social Disorders caused by fear, and insecurity

- Obsessive-Compulsive Disorders, Addictive Behaviors

- Self-defeating Behaviors

- Autism

- Tourette's Syndrome

There are many other psychological disorders, but those are just a few. If you examine the curses in Deuteronomy 28, it lists confusion, madness of heart, emotional and mental torment, spiritual blindness, spiritual oppression, being driven to insanity and utter ruin. That encompasses a great deal that could come under some sort of a curse. These are also what I believe to be destroyer spirits released into a person's life.

This is not to say that chemical imbalances in the brain cannot be one of the causes — however, it takes discernment and wisdom in partnership with Holy Spirit to correctly identify the cause of an issue, and that should be anyone's first step in obtaining an accurate diagnosis.

Demons, disorders and what is known as Arrested Development can enter a family through generational curses, unconfessed sin (which results in a guilty conscience and a lack of peace), rebellion, stubbornness, strong self-will (a form of idolatry) and childhood trauma.

With some people, there may be an obstinate, fighting and arguing spirit that rises up and insists on having things their way or a tantrum ensues. The individual finds it impossible to adapt to normal social situations. Others tend to withdraw and avoid contact with others because it creates fear and anxiety.

At the root of many of these issues is a spirit of fear. Fear of embarrassment, fear of rejection, fear of failure or fear of losing control can cause people to regress. Fear, anxiety, and stress are at the root of all of the issues mentioned in the list of social, physical and emotional disorders. FEAR is a spirit, not just an emotion. Fear does not come from God.

1 Sam. 16:14-16	Evil spirits cause terror.
1 Sam. 18:10-11;	Evil spirits are allowed by God due to a person's disobedience and sin.
1 Sam. 19:9,10;	
Matt. 18:33-35	
Mark 5:5; Matt. 17:15	Evil spirits cause lunacy and mental illness.
Mark 9:18-20	Evil spirits cause seizures.
Luke 13:11	Evil spirits cause sickness and a bent spine.
1 John 4:18	Evil spirits cause fear of torment and punishment.

| 2 Tim. 1:7 | "God has not given us a spirit of fear, but of power, love and a sound mind." |

Many individuals with social, psychological and neurological issues also report obsessive thoughts dealing with lust, sex, death, compulsive thoughts and other things that speak of immorality and uncleanness. In years past, these things were considered evidence of a weakened neurological system due to sin in the ancestry of a family line. In today's society and culture, sin is more widely accepted as normal, and other explanations are adopted to explain mental and emotional issues.

Some of the characteristics of certain issues/disorders (such as Tourette's, Oppositional Defiance Disorder and others) seem to manifest not at random moments but specifically at the most inopportune moments that bring shame, embarrassment, more fear, anxiety and social rejection towards those dealing with the problem. This suggests that those types of manifestations are calculated by something with an intelligent mind and purposeful agenda, not just a random happening.

Some individuals who deal with mental and emotional issues also report hearing voices, being given orders, or an uncontrollable need to act on the feeling that rises up inside of them. This suggests they are not in control of themselves, but they are more like a puppet where something else is directing and controlling their actions. Arrested Development is not just a disorder; it can also be a grouping of demonic spirits that attack the soul of an individual.

Revelation chapter 9 reveals the prince of demons from the bottomless pit (also called The Abyss) that is chief over a class of demons known as destroyer spirits. The name of this spirit is Apollyon, which means 'destroyer' or 'destruction.'

| Rev. 9:1-2 | "And the fifth angel blew his trumpet, and I saw a star fallen from heaven to earth, and he was given the key of the shaft of the bottomless pit; he opened the shaft of the bottomless pit and from the shaft rose smoke like the smoke of a great furnace, and the sun and the air were darkened with the smoke from the shaft," RSV. |

| Rev. 9:11 | "They have as king over them the angel of the abyss; his name in Hebrew is Abaddon, in the Greek, he has the name Apollyon." |

There is nothing more destructive than mental pain and emotional torment. As is noted in Revelation 9:3, destroyer spirits are assigned to torment people but not always kill them. These spirits resemble locusts, but sting like a scorpion and inflict mental anguish. During the years that I struggled with mental and emotional torment, I wanted to die, but God wouldn't allow it. I was literally sabotaging my life from every angle and couldn't seem to stop.

I overdosed repeatedly and came close to death many times, but God continued to spare me. I knew I had some unseen force in my life trying to destroy me, but I didn't know how to stop it. I am convinced that I was dealing with the spirit of Apollyon and many others. My life was full of fear. A form of mental torment is at the root of all of the disorders listed in the last couple of pages. When a person's mind is under attack, so is their self-esteem, their identity, and their future. Mental torment is the reason people commit suicide and do unexplained things to themselves and others. Every battle the enemy wages against mankind first starts in the mind.

When children experience fear, trauma, abuse, neglect, anxiety or some type of situation that opens the door to demonic oppression, evil spirits can attack them in their soul. Children are unaware that they are vulnerable, and most have no knowledge or understanding of spiritual warfare. They depend on the adults in their life for their safety and protection, and that includes taking authority over any spirits that may have taken up residence in that child's life. When the adults fail to take spiritual authority over evil spirits, or don't know which ones to address, those spirits stay and begin to release torment to the child's soul. This can result in Arrested Development, preventing people from growing into maturity. These spirits work to keep people stuck in emotional immaturity, and part of that is also blame shifting. The person refuses to take responsibility for their own faults and shifts the blame onto others for the problems they have created in life. It can be closely related to self-pity.

Some learning disabilities and slowed mental processes can also be attributed to Arrested Development. A person with a learning disability experiences something that causes the brain to block learning. Sometimes, these things come under the category of strongholds. It is just another attack on the soul because the individual that is affected suffers from embarrassment, discouragement and the constant fear of failure, especially surrounded by a person's peers. This can cause social rejection and critical judgments that cause a person to internalize shame.

Children can become stagnant in their learning processes and unable to progress normally. This can lead to doubt, uncertainty, double-mindedness, insecurity, inferiority and unbelief, making it difficult for the person to develop any real sense of faith. All of these things together can produce individuals that feel rejected, unworthy, defective, insecure, withdrawn or outcasts.

Arrested Development also manifests in areas where the person cannot hold down a job or maintain a sense of stability in their life. The person may look grown up on the outside but on the inside, they cannot deal with the issues of being an adult. They still think like a child and have immature emotional responses. Facing the real world as an adult is too stressful for them. They don't want the responsibility and look for ways to retreat.

My own father was a paranoid schizophrenic, and it was said that the pressure of having to take responsibility for a family is what triggered his emotional instability and downward path into mental illness. I'm not sure if that is accurate or not, but he certainly did retreat from any form of responsibility. He was so overcome with fear and anxiety that he convinced himself he was an invalid.

When you consider the issues at the heart of addicts, homelessness, mental issues, parental abandonment, and broken families, many of them are dealing with some of these problems yet don't know how to break the cycle, so the cycles continue to repeat into future generations. This produces generational poverty, brokenness, addictions and mental disorders.

People that struggle with Arrested Development feel insecure and lack confidence in their ability to live as a mature adult. They prefer to act as a child instead of taking responsibility for their lives, and many get stuck somewhere in adolescence. They would rather regress into childish behaviors or activities rather than do what is more appropriate for their age level.

When people are labeled and get used to the thought that they cannot do certain things for themselves, they begin to depend on others around them to do things for them that they should be doing for themselves. This can create co-dependency upon others that are not healthy. It also serves to keep people in an immature state of being. The Bible offers us clear instructions that we are to grow into adulthood and put away childish things. When a person is emotionally stuck, you can't talk about spiritual things because of the immaturity level.

1 Cor. 13:11   "When I was a child, I spoke like a child, I thought like a child, I reasoned like a child. When I became a man, I gave up childish ways."

1 Cor. 14:20   "Brothers, stop thinking like children. In regard to evil, be infants, but in your thinking, be mature."

When people reach adult age, they should live as adults. However, if there are mental and emotional blocks that are held in place by spiritual oppression, it can keep people from growing up. Arrested Development will cause people to make foolish, selfish decisions like an adolescent, without thought of consequences. Some people cannot grow up spiritually, either. They go through the motions of Christianity but never really grow in Christ.

Demonic spirits of Arrested Development work against the emotional, spiritual and natural growth of a person. Sometimes the individual can get caught up in sabotaging their own future because of the lies in their belief system. They are afraid of responsibility and success, and though they may want it, they often do things to trip themselves up so that they cannot make any real progress in their life.

Self-sabotage is a very real thing, but it can be overcome by heeding the Word of the LORD. Self-sabotage comes from an unstable mindset that is rooted in fear. Many things that have been wrongly diagnosed as psychological disorders, mental diseases and disorders can be healed through prayer and guidance from Holy Spirit.

BUILD YOUR HOUSE ON THE ROCK!

Matt. 7:24-27　"Everyone then who hears these words of mine and does them will be like a wise man who built his house on the rock. And the rain fell, and the floods came, and the winds blew and beat on that house, but it did not fall, because it had been founded on the rock. And everyone who hears these words of mine and does not do them will be like a foolish man who built his house on the sand. And the rain fell, and the floods came, and the winds blew and beat against that house, and it fell, and great was the fall of it."

YOU ARE THE HOUSE!

What are you building your life upon? Are you building your house upon your own wisdom or the wisdom of God? God's word is a guide to help us have wisdom for our lives and keep us from the things that will release destructive forces in our lives.

Jesus said that those that heard His word but didn't incorporate obedience to His Word into their lives would be like the unstable house built upon the sand. When the storms of life come, will your house stand, or will your foundation be washed away by the floods? You cannot build upon instability, but you can build upon the rock of Jesus Christ. When you have His presence in your life, it gives you peace of mind, self-control and stability. Fear always causes instability!

Ask: "God, what are the core issues of my life? What fears are controlling my behaviors?"

WISDOM TO DEFEAT THE ENEMY

Every lie comes from the Father of Lies. God's word is the truth! Satan has had many years of trying to deceive us, and he knows every place where he has twisted our belief system around dark deceptions. The enemy is just waiting for us to choose the path of self-sabotage so that he can keep us bound to the same old cycles that end in defeat, discouragement, and disappointment.

If people are to break free from repeating old cycles, then they need to first understand that demonic oppression, torment and curses are real. Lack of knowledge can destroy us. When a person has demonic attachments to their life, those spirits act like invisible magnets to other spirits. That is why people feel 'drawn' to other people that they may realize are not necessarily good for them, but they can't seem to break the magnetic power that keeps them connected to the wrong people. Demonic spirits have the assignment to pull people back into familiar territory, repeating the same habitual patterns and behaviors that result in brokenness.

The only way to break the cycle is to choose to be uncomfortable because being uncomfortable is the pathway to change. God wants us to find our stability in Him.

Is. 33:5-6   "The Lord is exalted, for He dwells on high; He has filled Zion with justice and righteousness. Wisdom and knowledge shall be the stability of your times and the strength of salvation. The fear of the Lord is His treasure."

PRAYER

Father,

I thank you for opening my eyes to see my own blind spots.

Help me understand the root issues of my life and what lies are tied to my belief system.

Holy Spirit, lead me into the truth that will set me free. Help me choose the path and the plan you have for me, even if it is uncomfortable.

Take my hand and walk me through the fear.

Bring me out to the other side.

On behalf of my own sin and those in my generational line, I renounce and confess the sins of idolatry and rebellion.

Forgive us for adopting false gods and demonic spirits to lead our lives. I renounce and confess the sins of allowing other masters besides you to be lord over my life.

I confess and renounce the sins of evil speaking, shedding innocent blood, slander, lying, bearing false witness against others, dissension and causing division, and pride and haughty attitudes.

I apply the Blood of Jesus over every sin in my generational line; those committed by my ancestors and those committed by myself. I ask You, O God, to cleanse us from all unrighteousness and forgive our sins.

You know and discern heart and motive better than I. You know those relationships in my life that are unhealthy. Some have been established by the enemy to strip me of all spiritual strength.

I ask You to take those relationships out of my hands and do what you know needs to be done with them.

I forgive anyone the enemy used to speak a false, negative judgment over my life. I condemn those words and command them to bear no more fruit in Jesus's name. I ask You, Father, to remove all false labels from my soul and please speak Your life-giving affirmations over me now.

Help me, Holy Spirit, to hear what my Father speaks about me and to receive those loving words in faith.

I renounce and break all agreement with spirits of sabotage and command them to leave me now in Jesus's name.

I declare a disentanglement and separation from all relationships that are designed to destroy, hinder, sabotage, and undermine my identity in Christ, and those that have set themselves against the anointing, calling and purposes of God in Jesus's name.

I submit to the authority of Your Holy Spirit, and I renounce the spirits of fear, insecurity and inferiority. I command them to go from me now and return to the abyss.

I resist all lying and familiar spirits and bind them to silence. I command them to return to where they came from in Jesus's name.

I resist and break agreements with pride, resentment, unforgiveness, bitterness, self-pity, stubbornness, rebellion, unbelief, regret, and the spirit of the past. I command them to leave me now and return to the place created for them in Jesus's name.

I break the power of fear that came in as a result of trauma and indoctrination into occult rituals in Jesus's name.

I choose to see myself as victorious, not a victim, and I command all predatory spirits that cause victimization to leave me now in Jesus's name.

I choose to forgive anyone who has hurt me or caused trauma to my life, and I release them to You now, Father, for You are a God of justice. I trust You to oversee justice in my life as well as in the lives of those who have caused me pain.

I repent for complaining, murmuring and criticisms that have opened the door to a spirit of death and destruction.

I condemn the words I've spoken over myself and others, and I pray that the fruit of negative words would fall to the ground without bearing any evil fruit.

I choose to be grateful, LORD. I thank You for all that You are doing in my life to release my restoration.

As I submit to the authority of the Lord Jesus Christ and the authority of His Holy Spirit, I now command all evil princes, deputies and wardens, as well as those known as Arrested Development, to leave me now and return to the abyss in Jesus's name. You must leave me now and never return.

I reject and resist all destroyer spirits from the bottomless pit and their chief prince Apollyon. Let the strongmen known as Apollyon, Arrested Development, Fear and Satan be bound and rendered completely immobile, in the name of Jesus Christ. Return to where you came from and never torment me again.

I declare that I will not submit myself to the spirit of fear in Jesus's name. I will not think as a child or act as a child. I choose to grow into spiritual and emotional maturity.

I declare the enemy's plans are ruined as of this day, and no weapon formed against me shall prosper, according to Isaiah 54:17.

I declare I am anointed with fresh oil, as it is written in Psalm 92:10.

Thank You, Father, for releasing the joy of the LORD to be my strength. Give me victory over the enemy, and help me to walk in the light of Your truth. In Jesus's name. Amen.

TOXIC THINKING

Strongholds in our thought processes produce toxic emotions. Toxic emotions cause us to meditate upon hurtful words, and negative memories, and rehearse a variety of negative conversations, either in our own head or the actual words we speak. Toxic thinking can produce all manner of physical ills, stress, and mental health issues.

The only way to detoxify the mind is to renew it. Romans 12:2 reminds us to "be transformed by the renewing of our mind."

How do you know if you have toxic thoughts?

1. Do you catch yourself replaying a conversation or event that happened in the past, wishing you could have said or done something differently?

2. Do you find yourself thinking about someone you dislike, rehearsing what you would say to them if you bumped into them?

3. Do you find yourself worrying about the future or events that have not yet occurred?

4. Do you find yourself overreacting and jumping to a negative conclusion before you know all the facts about a situation?

5. Do you find yourself being critical or judgmental towards others or speaking negatively towards other people, such as in gossip or slander?

6. Do you find yourself engaging in petty behaviors such as belittling others, tearing people down, or unloading guilt, condemnation or shame on others to make yourself feel better?

7. Do you feel the need to control others?

8. Do you struggle with forgiveness issues?

9. Do you feel like a victim of circumstance or that you lack the ability to take control of your life?

10. Be honest. Have you made self-pity your friend instead of your foe? Have you embraced feeling sorry for yourself?

11. Do you find yourself making negative, condemning statements about yourself?

12. Do you find yourself having regret over past decisions and situations, wishing you could go back and change them?

13. Do you feel as if you are stuck in your past and cannot get free from it?

14. Do you fail to set healthy boundaries with others and allow others to take advantage of you?

15. Do you say yes when you wish you could say no, taking on false burdens in order to please others?

16. Do you find yourself struggling with inner resentment towards others?

17. Do you find yourself perpetually distracted with negative thoughts?

18. Do you struggle with fear, worry, and anxiety?

19. Do you feel jealous or insecure?

20. Is your mind filled with suspicion or accusation towards others?

If you answered yes to some of these questions, you have toxic thinking. At the root of all toxic thinking is unbelief. These negative thoughts will contribute to stress, strain, and wear down your body's defenses. It will also steal your peace and joy, and sabotage your future. The only way to change toxic thought patterns is to recognize them, renounce them, and ask God to help you develop new, healthy thought processes.

PRAYER

Father God,

I repent for toxic thinking. Forgive me for departing from the faith and having an unbelieving mind. I renounce fear, anxiety, and worry. I renounce a critical, judgmental spirit, the spirit of jealousy, suspicion, insecurity and accusation. I renounce the spirit of self-pity, and the lie that I am a victim of the past or negative circumstances. I renounce the spirits of regret and the past. I renounce toxic shame, embarrassment, inferiority, and insecurity and ask for healing for my emotional wounds. I renounce the spirit of Leviathan, stubbornness, defensiveness and pride. I say to the strongmen, be bound in Jesus's name. Let all the works of the enemy be unraveled, and may the ultimate strongman, Satan, be bound in the name and authority of the Lord Jesus Christ.

I renounce and repent for any obsessive thoughts, fantasy thinking, condemnation, rejection, anger and bitterness. I command those spirits to leave me now and return to the abyss that was created for them. I repent for making pride my walls of defense, and I tell the walls to come down in my heart and mind right now in Jesus's name.

I tell the spirit of shame, rage, dishonor, disrespect, disappointment and disapproval to be still, be bound, and leave me now in the name and authority of the Lord Jesus Christ.

I break any and all agreements that were made with these spirits and command them to leave me now in the name and authority of the Lord Jesus Christ.

I repent for holding resentment, grudges, unforgiveness and condemnation toward others. I ask Your forgiveness, Father, for evil speaking, slander, gossip, and word curses I have released over myself and others. I condemn those words and submit them to the Lord Jesus in obedience, asking Him to apply the blood of Jesus to my sin.

I thank you, Jesus, for cleansing me of all unrighteousness. I bless those I have spoken ill about. (Be specific – name the individuals and ask God to bless them in all the ways you would like to be blessed).

I bless myself, too, and ask that You help me to speak what is right, pure and wholesome. Cleanse my heart from wickedness, unbelief and toxic thoughts. I break any negative soul ties with anyone that has caused me to feel covered in toxic shame. I send any fragmented parts of their soul back to them, and I call for any fragmented parts of my soul to come back to me, in Jesus's name. Thank you for healing and restoring my soul. Amen.

CHAPTER FIVE
SOUL TIES

The Bible doesn't use the term 'soul tie,' but it does speak of souls being knit together. It speaks of what links souls together in the spiritual realm. There can be good spiritual bonds, such as man and wife, that are committed to one another in marriage. This is what is meant by two souls becoming one. The heart, mind and soul are all involved in a marriage covenant, just as we are also commanded to love the Lord with all our heart, with all our soul, and all our mind. (ref. Matt.22:37)

A marriage involves every part of both people. There is either sex within the confines of marriage, which God has said is a good thing, or there is sex outside of marriage, which is sin. In a marriage relationship, the physical act of sexual relations binds the two souls together, but it's much more than that. A godly union between a man and a woman involves their spirits becoming intertwined. It is the soul and spirit of one person touching the soul and spirit of another person. This is essentially exactly what defines worship. It is the deep, intimate connection – spirit to spirit – with God. Mingling spirit to spirit is an act of worship. Thus, a godly marriage is consecrated to the Lord and therefore becomes an extension of our relationship with God.

A soul tie can also be formed through sexual relations outside of marriage, but that forms an ungodly soulish bond with the other person. Do you wonder why you cannot stop thinking about someone from your past? Do you wonder why your heart seems discontent or you have a wandering eye, even though you try to remain faithful in your relationship? Do you feel unable to make a commitment to a relationship, always thinking the 'grass is greener on the other side,' or that you might miss out on someone better? These are all symptomatic of a person with an unhealthy soul.

There is no blessing from God on sex outside of covenant, because as stated above, mingling one spirit with another is a form of worship. Who is getting the glory? With whom are you in the covenant? It is either God or Satan, and that makes all the difference between whether or not there is a blessing or propensity towards spiritual oppression. People with a promiscuous lifestyle of casual sex without discrimination often have a hard time bonding with anyone because they end up giving away pieces of their soul to everyone they sleep with. They become spiritually polluted.

1 Cor. 6:16   "Do you not know that he who unites himself with a prostitute is one with her in body? For it is said, "The two will become one flesh.""

Part of this is because sexual relations with other people is a bit like becoming contaminated with an STD (sexually transmitted disease), only in the spiritual sense. Sex is not just a physical act; it is also a spiritual act. People become vulnerable and exposed to whatever they and their other partner(s) have been in contact with. It works like this in the spiritual realm, too.

Whatever spirits have been in the lives of you and your sexual partners can infect both of you with unclean spirits. Sex outside of marriage is a sin, so if a person has committed this sin and never repented from it, those demons have been granted legal grounds to be in their life.

Most people never stop to think about this sort of thing, and they have no idea why they can't make relationships work. While part of that may be due to other factors, it could also be because spirits influence both sides of the relationship. Those things can still be a factor that affects other relationships until confession and repentance takes place. Demonic spirits must be told to leave. That is why God designed marriage to be a mutual covenant, not just casual sex. His rules are there to protect us. When our relationships honor God, they receive a blessing of strength, unity, and the protection of that union.

Mark 10:7-9   "For this reason, a man will leave his father and mother and be united to his wife, [a] and the two will become one flesh.'[b] So they are no longer two, but one flesh. 9 Therefore, what God has joined together, let no one separate."

"Whenever a person is sexually involved with another person, neurochemical changes occur in both their brains that encourage limbic, emotional bonding. Limbic bonding is the reason casual sex doesn't really work for most people on a whole mind and body level. Two people may decide to have sex 'just for the fun of it,' yet something is occurring on another level that they might not have decided on at all: sex is enhancing an emotional bond between them whether they want it or not. One person, often the woman, is bound to form an attachment and will be hurt when a casual affair ends. One reason it is usually the woman who is hurt most is that the female limbic system is larger than the males." – Dr. Daniel Amen, from his book, *Change Your Brain, Change Your Life.*

Kris Vollatton, in his article "*7 Signs of an Unhealthy Soul Tie*" writes, "Unhealthy soul ties are often the ramifications of having partners that you create a life-long bond with through a sexual encounter(s), but with whom you only have a short-term relationship with. The bond (soul tie) remains long after the relationship is over, leaving both sexual partners longing for wholeness."[7] Soul ties can make people feel as though their souls are knit together with another person.

Soul ties aren't just the result of a sexual union. One such example in the Bible is the friendship between Jonathan and David. In spite of King Saul repeatedly trying to kill his up-and-coming replacement to the throne, Jonathan and David's friendship flourished. These were two men that had an incredibly strong bond and were committed to one another. Jonathan realized David would one day be king and instead of trying to sabotage him, Jonathan supported David and made a covenant agreement with him.

1 Sam. 18:1   "And it came to pass, when he had made an end of speaking unto Saul, that the soul of Jonathan was knit with the soul of David, and Jonathan loved him as his own soul."

2 Sam. 1:26   "I am distressed for you, my brother Jonathan; how very pleasant have you been to me; your love to me was extraordinary, surpassing the love of women."

There can also be other forms of soul ties, such as:

- A dysfunctional bond to an abuser (a pimp, molester, rape, verbal or physical abuser).
- A bond formed through a traumatic event.
- An intimate bond, such as what twins form for one another in the womb.
- Soul ties with family, friends or other Christians.
- Between a pastor and his flock/congregation members.
- Negative soul ties formed through idolatry or unhealthy obsessions.
- Demonic soul ties through Satanic Ritual Abuse or involvement in the occult.
- Controlling relationships.
- Fantasies, fantasy play, video games, drugs and other forms of false comfort.

Inner vows and agreements also bind the soul. Examples: "I will always love you," or "I will never love another man/woman" - that is a vow that needs to be broken. When agreements have been made verbally, they need to be renounced through confession and prayer. Examples:

Num. 30:2-4   "If a man makes a vow to the LORD or swears an oath to obligate himself by a pledge, he must not break his word; he must do everything he has promised. And if a woman in

---

[7] Vallotton, Chris: "7 Signs of an Unhealthy Soul Tie," May 3, 2019, https://krisvallotton.com/7-signs-of-an-unhealthy-soul-tie/

her father's house during her youth makes a vow to the LORD or obligates herself by a pledge, and her father hears about her vow or pledge but says nothing to her, all the vows and pledges with which she has bound herself shall stand ... " Berean Study Bible.

Acts 23:12   "And when it was day, certain of the Jews banded together, and bound themselves under a curse, saying that they would neither eat nor drink till they had killed Paul ... ."

Matt. 5:33   "Again, you have heard that it was said to the ancients, 'Do not break your oath, but fulfill your vows to the Lord.'"

Judges 11:35   "As soon as Jephthah saw her, he tore his clothes and said, "No! Not my daughter! You have brought me to my knees! You have brought great misery upon me, for I have given my word to the LORD and cannot take it back."

Ungodly soul ties are formed in the mind, heart and emotions of a person, which can cause them to be overcome with thoughts of another person. Ungodly soul ties are formed when people are emotionally needy for love, affection or affirmation. It is often a co-dependent relationship.

The soul should never be the dominant leader in any relationship. Instead, we should be led by the Spirit of God. A soul tie can cause a person to feel the emotions, personal struggles and soulish issues that are taking place in the person with whom they are connected. Sometimes it can even feel as though your own soul is dying. One person can begin to take on the personality of the other person and lose themselves in the relationship. They allow their own personality to become completely absorbed by the more dominant personality.

When a spirit of witchcraft is involved, as in a spirit with a Jezebel assignment or someone very dominating, a person may find themselves being utterly controlled by a stronger personality type and sacrificing their convictions because of the unpredictable and abusive personality of another person.

You may find yourself unnaturally attracted to someone you instinctually understand to be wrong for you, but you can't stop thinking about them. You are drawn to the wrong person but can't break the emotional bond, even though you know the person or relationship is unhealthy. This is often an indicator of a spirit of witchcraft present in the life of one or both individuals, trying to form an unhealthy, demonic attachment. This is an assignment from the enemy to keep a person bound to brokenness so that they cannot receive the true mate God has for them.

Soul ties can also be formed with overbearing or abusive spiritual leaders.

BREAKING SOUL TIES

Ask Holy Spirit to bring to mind anyone with whom you may have formed a soul tie, and write it down. Write down any feelings you experienced in regard to each person. Was there emotional wounding? If so, write down what you felt you lost in that relationship. Do you still need to forgive them? If you did wrong things towards others, write them down and acknowledge them.

Ask Holy Spirit to remind you of any vows or agreements you made with each person.

1. How did each relationship affect your identity, self-esteem and self-respect?

2. Did any of those relationships damage or distort your ability to trust your discernment and ability to make wise decisions?

Now, go down your list and begin to speak to the Lord about each area, confessing your sin and applying the blood of Jesus to them. Repent for opening the door to sin that gave the enemy legal rights to your life. Ask Holy Spirit to heal any emotional wounding and to restore any areas of your heart and soul that were damaged. Ask God to restore anything you feel you lost in those relationships. Forgive those that hurt or disappointed you. Forgive them for any lingering feelings of rejection and let them off the hook. They are no longer in your life for a reason! Sometimes the wrong people need to exit before God can release what He has for you. If you did anything wrong in retaliation, ask God to forgive you for those things.

Renounce any vows or agreements you made that would form a soul tie with that person(s), placing them under the blood of Jesus. Be specific.

Renounce any agreements you have made with spirits of rejection, shame, self-rejection and self-hatred, inferiority, insecurity, abandonment, lust, sexual confusion, abuse, perversion, incubus and succubus spirits, promiscuity, the spirit of adultery and whoredom, unclean spirits. Send them back to the pit of hell in the name and authority of the Lord Jesus Christ.

Ask God to restore any areas of your soul that were lost according to His promise in Psalm 23:3.

CHAPTER SIX
TOXIC SHAME

Toxic shame is like a worm that buries itself deep within the mind and eats away at the individual's sense of identity and self-esteem. It hides in a person's subconscious affecting their belief system. Normally, shame is a response to feeling guilty about some negative action or a poor decision. It's a momentary thing that passes after an event has ended and the person deals with the situation or event. Toxic shame, however, is buried in the subconscious and doesn't go away. It is like a personal broadcast system that constantly sends out lies and negative messages. Only the recipient can hear the subliminal messages that are aimed at destroying their identity and self-esteem.

Parents that carry toxic shame will pass it on to their children unless they get healed and delivered. A child that is abused (mentally, emotionally, physically or sexually) has no way of neutralizing painful words or actions that are harmful to them. They are vulnerable and are dependent upon the adults in their lives to foster a sense of safety, nurturing and a loving environment. If any of those elements are missing or violated, all they can do is form a defense against the external factors that are perceived as a threat, or they internalize the emotions and reactions that are in their environment.

When a child feels neglected, for instance, the irritability, disinterest, or emotional detachment from their parents or caregivers translates to a message, "I am invisible – no one sees me," or "I am not loveable," and makes room for the conclusion, "therefore, I must be unimportant." This opens the door for the spirit of rejection to attach to the child, reinforcing the lie. Parents that lean towards high expectations of perfectionism are harsh in their verbal correction, or are strict authoritarians. They often place a higher priority on obedience than nurturing in love.

This tends to make a child feel attacked in their personhood and unable to meet the expectations of others. Therefore, the child feels they can never measure up to an acceptable standard. Their identity becomes rooted in rejection and unworthiness, and the need to feel loved and accepted becomes conditional, based on performance, forcing them to adopt perfectionism as a means of striving to obtain validation and acceptance.

Rejection is tied to insecurity and a sense of inferiority. The person feels defective as a human being and begins to agree with the lies of the enemy. The individual that suffers from toxic shame cannot differentiate between a negative action they've done from the feeling that they are inherently bad. A feeling of unworthiness, insecurity and inferiority begins to shape the person's character, behavior and the way they interact with others.

Toxic shame is related to how people feel about themselves. Therefore, the fear of abandonment or rejection is present and becomes a spiritually-rooted issue in the child's life. This is one of the factors that cause the orphan spirit. A person that suffers from toxic shame has experienced feelings of being a disappointment to others, and a sense of disapproval, causing them resentment and fear of rejection. Their inner critic tells them they are unable to please the important people in their lives (usually caregivers, parents or other close relationships), which can cause rebellion and other negative responses. It's a defense mechanism to try to deal with underlying shame and unhealthy emotions. Harsh attitudes toward themselves deeply impact a person's self-image.

When a person suffers from toxic shame, the fear of experiencing more shame causes them to establish fortified walls of defense. The person may attempt to block a perceived situation where they feel they might experience shame, rejection, or disrespect; however, it's often an irrational reaction rooted in the subconscious. Their actions often serve to provoke a corresponding adverse response in others, resulting in the opposite outcome of what they tried to prevent.

Before you know it, a battle can ensue, all because the person with toxic shame was trying to protect themselves from feeling unpleasant, negative, shame-based emotions. The enemy's lie reinforces subliminal messages in the person's internal broadcasting system, telling them that they are defective, unloved, or unworthy of being treated with respect and dignity. The enemy rejoices in the dysfunction, of course, and loves to keep the cycle of co-dependency, strife, depression and toxic emotions alive. This sort of negative response can sabotage relationships, future opportunities and a healthy, peaceful life unless it is surrendered to Christ for their healing. Healing emotions and memories is a deeper work that will be addressed later in this book.

In other cases, some children become withdrawn, shy, or insecure because they don't trust others or social situations. Toxic shame is the result of parents or others that constantly reinforce the idea of disappointment and disapproval. It could be a teacher, a boss, a co-worker or some other situation that leaves a person feeling humiliated, ashamed, belittled, betrayed and insecure. Criticisms, corrections, and the constant sense of being picked at can cause a person of any age to withdraw and shut down in an attempt at self-preservation.

A more passive person may tend to become a poor communicator or allow themselves to be bullied, but a different personality type may lean towards anger, aggression and resentment. Neither person in that sort of situation can develop a healthy sense of intimacy or communication in relationships because they are afraid of allowing themselves to feel vulnerable.

All these factors can cause the victim of toxic shame to make bitter root judgments about those inflicting the pain and shame. It can also contribute to people making internal vows that reinforce the negative emotions connected to toxic thinking. Some examples of toxic thinking and inner vows are:

"I am no good. I always make mistakes. It is safer to just not try to do anything."

"Nobody loves me. Even God has abandoned me. I cannot trust anyone."

"My mother/father/grandparent doesn't love me. They think I can't do anything right. I will always be a failure. I will never trust them again."

"I am so tired of being put down and rejected. I will never let anyone hurt me again."

"I will never trust an authority figure again."

"My father is always busy with work. I will never choose work over family."

"I will never let anyone close to me again. I will never allow myself to be vulnerable again."

"I will never let anyone love me again."

"I will never amount to anything. I will never be financially safe."

"I will not cry again."

"I cannot trust anyone. I will not let anyone control me."

"I will not forgive ___ unless they ___."

"I will prove I am not worthless."

"I will make them respect me."

"I will not ask for help from anyone again."

"All men/women are alike. I will always be suspicious. I will monitor everything they do."

"I will never allow myself to feel pain like that again. I will guard my emotions."

"I will never allow myself to need anyone again. I will take care of myself."

WISDOM TO DEFEAT THE ENEMY

"I will protect my own heart."

"I will leave the relationship before they can hurt me."

"My spouse has hurt me for the last time. I refuse to love them."

"I will not let ____ get away with offending me. I will give them a piece of my mind."

"I am fat. I have to purge to get my weight under control."

"Only thin people are attractive. I will starve myself until I am accepted and attractive."

PRAYER

Dear Heavenly Father,

I realize that I have believed many lies and carried toxic thinking with me for a long time. I allowed pain, disappointment, feelings of rejection and other negative emotions to cause me to make ungodly vows. Forgive me, Lord, for the idolatry of trusting in myself to keep me safe rather than trusting You with my heart. I am not able to prevent myself from experiencing hurt. That is a part of life that I know I must accept. I reject the lie that the inner vows I made during a time when I felt vulnerable and in pain would somehow keep me safe. Forgive me for not fully trusting You with my heart. I bring my heart to you as an offering and place it in your hands.

These vows and wrong beliefs have hardened my heart and caused me to feel alienated from You and others. Please forgive me for making wrong judgments, for feeling distrustful of others, and believing the lies the enemy told me. The enemy has formed assignments against me and released curses in my life, but as I now submit to the authority of Your Holy Spirit, I declare that I break all agreements that I made with spirits of darkness, and I cancel all assignments and curses that the kingdom of darkness has used against me.

In the name of the Lord Jesus Christ, I break every spoken or inner vow, and I repent for making ungodly judgments. I repent of the sin of unbelief, trusting in my own strength, and creating barriers to my own healing. Please let the blood of Jesus be applied to every sin, transgression and iniquity, including those of my ancestors that may also have resulted in betrayal, broken trust, broken vows and covenants, and the pain that led people in my family line to make the wrong sort of vows and oaths. This resulted in bitterness, and allowed unbelief, rebellion, witchcraft and control to release curses in my family.

Father, please restore any relationships that You want restored in my life. Heal my perspective, help me to have humility and confess my sins so that I may be healed, and the important relationships in my life can be healed and restored. Remind me to share these truths with others so they can receive their freedom also and come back into the right relationship with you. I ask for Your wisdom, guidance and direction to show me any steps You want me to take. I submit my thoughts, memories and emotions to the authority of Your Holy Spirit, and I yield myself to You. Thank you for releasing healing and freedom in Jesus's name. Amen.

IDENTIFYING TOXIC THOUGHTS TOWARD GOD

Unfortunately, parents and other authority figures in a person's life transfer over to how a person perceives God. It can cause a person to feel offended towards the Lord because they have chosen to hold God accountable for some pain or disappointment in their life. God does not make mistakes, and He does not need our forgiveness. We need His forgiveness. Sometimes people allow the accuser (Satan) to influence them and accuse God of being unfair. Some lies a person might be tempted to believe are:

i)   My heavenly Father is absent from my life. He deserted me when I needed Him most.

ii) God doesn't care about me. He never answers my prayers.

iii) I can never seem to please God. He demands perfection and I'm not perfect, so He must not love me. I am not good enough to earn God's love."

iv) God doesn't want me to have any enjoyment in life. He is too rigid and wants me to live a boring life. Who wants to serve a God like that?

v)   I can't trust God. He let me down when He did not answer my prayer for ___."

vi) I can't hear God speak. Why do other people say they can hear Him but I can't? He must not want to talk to me.

vii) God is abusive and mean. The Old Testament stories prove He is unloving and punishing. Why would I want to make him my God?

viii) God doesn't exist. I don't need to obey the Bible. That was written a long time ago, and those beliefs are not relevant for today."

ix) God allows evil to happen to innocent people. He must not be good if He lets evil and injustice happen, and people just get away with it.

All of these misconceptions about God can make it difficult for someone to develop intimacy with Him until they accept that they have believed lies. If a person is bitter about some situation in life then they will have a distorted perspective that makes it impossible for them to intimately know their Father. It also makes it difficult for the person to understand their own true identity because we are made in the image and likeness of God (ref. Gen. 1:27).

DIAGNOSING TOXIC SHAME

Here are the signs you will need to look out for:

1. Relationships are dysfunctional and often co-dependent.

2. The person struggles with addictions as coping mechanisms or to dull emotional pain.

3. Low self-esteem and feelings of unworthiness.

4. Perfectionism, or workaholic behaviors, strives to be affirmed through works or good deeds.

5. Feels unloved and rejected.

6. Struggles with insecurity and feelings of inferiority.

7. People pleaser. Takes on false burdens and obligations to be liked or accepted.

8. Victim mentality thinks of oneself as a martyr.

9. Bound by self-pity, self-righteousness or narcissism.

10. Blames everyone else for their misfortune or lack of fulfillment.

11. Impossible to please.

12. Harbors anger and resentment, quick to lose temper.

13. Scorns others, treats others with contempt, dishonor or disrespect. Belittling behaviors towards others.

14. Twists truth in order to make themselves a victim of other people's actions. Engages in blame shifting; refuses to take responsibility for their own toxic emotions and responses.

15. Bitter root judgments against others.

16. Leaves a trail of destruction behind them.

17. Feels paralyzed by insecurity or inability to make decisions.

18. Inability to form healthy relationships; cannot develop true intimacy.

19. Silence and secrecy attempt to cover their shame; fear of judgment keeps them from acknowledging their need for help.

20. Prone to criticism, judgment and evil speaking about others.

21. Isolated, lonely, withdrawn. Can feel suicidal and depressed, wanting to escape feelings of inadequacy, deep depression and avoid being with themselves.

22. Outward expression of rebellion and showing others they don't care about themselves. Such as deliberately failing in school or work, risk-taking behaviors, irresponsible behaviors, and lack of respect toward authority.

23. Cutting and other self-harm behaviors (manifestations of self-hatred and painful, destructive emotions).

24. Controlling, uses guilt and condemnation to emotionally manipulate others.

25. Self-sabotaging behaviors.

26. Settling for unfulfilling relationships or jobs based on low self-esteem.

27. Mental illness as a result of toxic thinking, such as mood swings, depression, emotional instability.

HOW TO HEAL FROM TOXIC SHAME

While it may take time to walk through the process, the good news is anyone can be healed and set free from toxic shame if they truly want to be healed. Nothing is impossible with God. Every negative emotion can be reversed. Every broken heart can be healed. It takes obedience and cooperation with the Holy Spirit, and no one promises that there won't be some pain along the way, but facing our pain is what helps us overcome it.

Shame cannot exist when it's met with compassion, vulnerability and transparency. It needs secrecy and silence to exist. Secrecy is to internalize feelings and keep it hidden, but silence is a bit different. Silence refers to a lack of repentance or acknowledgment that there is a deeply rooted issue in need of attention. When we share our stories with people who will not judge us or make us uncomfortable, the internal pressure of toxic emotions begins to subside.

It's like triggering the release valve on a pressure cooker. People need to find a safe place to be vulnerable. Then, when we confront shame with empathy instead of judgment and understanding instead of insensitive religious answers, the individual can finally connect with someone that can lead them to Jesus, where the power of toxic shame can finally be broken.

When facilitating a healing session, it is important that the individual understands the necessity of transparency and vulnerability so that Jesus and the Holy Spirit have full access to the person's heart, mind and memories. Ask the Holy Spirit to mediate and facilitate the healing session and bring to mind the memories of when shame was introduced into the person's life. How old were they?

Ask the Holy Spirit to help the person see the event as it unfolded or recall the memory. If you are dealing with childhood memories, these are questions that can be introduced. Always wait after asking a question and give the Holy Spirit time to show the individual important details before acknowledging those things and moving forward. Pray about each thing that is revealed and continue to ask questions. Here are some examples to keep in mind:

1. What did the child do?

2. What did others who were present do?

3. What happened to bring shame into the picture? How was the person/child devalued?

4. What judgments did the child make about themselves? What judgments did the child make about the adults that were present?

5. What did the child need at the time of the incident?

6. Where was Jesus at that moment? What does Jesus have to say about that event?

7. What lie did the enemy introduce at that time?

8. What is the truth? What does Jesus say about the child that experienced a negative or traumatic event?

Have the person renounce any lies they believed about themselves and repeat what Jesus says about their true identity. Give the person an opportunity to forgive those that hurt them, betrayed their trust, and shamed them. Break every agreement with toxic shame, disappointment, disapproval, anger, resentment, rejection and self-hatred. Renounce the lie that you were abandoned or rejected.

Send all evil spirits back to the pit of hell where they belong. Have the individual tell them to go in the name and authority of Jesus Christ. It is very important that the person takes authority over the spirits themselves! It is a show of force between them and the enemy to finally take a stand and exercise their authority in Christ.

Speak the truth over them and have them bless themselves. Give them words of affirmation and scriptures to speak over themselves. Tell the individual they are safe and can make new choices based on new information. They no longer have to feel victimized.

PRAYER

Father God,

I acknowledge that I have had toxic shame in my core beliefs that have made me agree with Satan's lies. I renounce every lie, agreement, covenant and inner vow that has yoked me to the enemy.

I repent for allowing myself to have a victim mentality and allowing self-pity to manipulate my emotions. I am not a victim; I am victorious in Christ. I renounce all distorted thinking about myself, and by faith, I receive the truth of Your word.

I repent for believing that you are someone. You are not, for accusing you of being unfair, harsh, unloving or difficult to please. I ask Your forgiveness for grieving your Holy Spirit and keeping You at a distance. Help me to draw closer to you, Father. I want to experience Your love in a deeper, more meaningful way.

I repent for having personally played any part in sabotaging my own life and for embracing wrong thoughts and beliefs.

I choose to forgive my parents and anyone else that has covered me in toxic shame. I forgive them for not meeting my emotional needs when I was a child and for making me feel unaccepted, insecure, unworthy and unloved. I forgive them for neglect, and making me feel unimportant. I forgive them for opening the door to the enemy. I realize that they could not affirm me in my true identity when they were also covered in toxic shame, and they could not nurture me or give me what I needed because of their own brokenness. I forgive them from my heart and cancel any judgments I have carried against them.

I forgive all other adults who have contributed to my feelings of shame, humiliation, rejection, embarrassment, or in some way devalued who I am as a person. I bless them and release them from the hurt they caused me. I realize they were a pawn, being used by Satan to inflict pain so that he could continue reinforcing his lies in my belief system.

I renounce spirits of disappointment, disapproval, disrespect and dishonor. I renounce anger, resentment, humiliation, inferiority, insecurity, shame and unforgiveness. I renounce perfectionism, unbelief, and abandonment. I bind these spirits and command them to leave me now and never return in Jesus's name.

I release my spirit to agree with the Spirit of Faith, Love, and Acceptance. I come into agreement with the truth that says I am loved, valued, esteemed, accepted and secure in my identity. I am a blood-bought, born-again child of God. Jesus assigned value to my life when He died on the cross for me. He was resurrected in victory, and that victory is transferred to me as well.

It is because of Jesus Christ that I am free to choose healing instead of brokenness. I choose forgiveness and mercy over judgment. I choose to let go of my pain and surrender it to the Lord. I choose to surrender shame and every other negative emotion and let it go so that I can live free from the enemy's lies. As a child of God, I get to choose to live life on my terms, not on the enemy's terms. Satan, take everything you have put on me and go! Never come back in Jesus's name!

I thank you, Jesus, that You are able to reverse every curse and restore every part of my soul that has been wounded or damaged. I thank You, Lord, for helping me bring every deep and hidden thing to light so that darkness loses its grip on me. I am grateful, Father, for Your Son that took the beating and the punishment on my behalf so that I can be healed. Thank You, Holy Spirit, for the continuous revelation that will lead me to deeper levels of truth, healing and freedom.

Father, I also ask Your forgiveness for any way that I have covered others in toxic shame. Forgive me for hurting (Be specific, name the individuals _____). Lord Jesus, help me to stop any cycles of brokenness and change the way I communicate so that I don't make victims of others. Pull out the evil roots of toxic shame, disappointment, disapproval, anger, resentment and unbelief. Anoint me to break the power of shame in others, Lord Jesus.

Don't let me do to others the things that have been done to me. I yield my heart and my responses to You, Holy Spirit. Put a guard against my lips so that I do not speak what is discouraging to others. Bless me with a clean heart and wholesome speech that is uplifting and encouraging to people. Let Your word be hidden in my heart so that I do not sin against you or others. In Jesus's name, amen.

CHAPTER SEVEN
SECRET ROOMS

There are various places in scripture that refer to our human body as either a house or a temple. Jesus referenced his body as the temple in John 2:19, and the Apostle Paul stated that we are the temple of the living God in 2 Corinthians 6:16. 2 Cor. 5:1 also references our earthly house or our body, so we see that in the New Testament, the temple where God dwells (the human body) is known as a house. In every 'house' there are many rooms.

If you notice the following scripture, it refers to our human body as a house where evil spirits can take up residence. Some versions of Luke 11:24 use the word 'dry,' and other versions use the term 'waterless places.' The demonic spirit that has been cast out of a person seeks rest. That is an interesting thought, is it not? What exactly causes a demon to feel at rest? The answer is contained in the scripture. It's a place that is dry, empty, and without the living water known as the infilling of the Holy Spirit. For a demon to feel 'at rest,' there must be a void that has not been filled with the presence of God.

Luke 11:24   "When the unclean spirit is gone out of a man, he walketh through dry places, seeking rest; and finding none, he saith, I will return unto my house whence I came out" KJV.

In scripture, the dry desert places were known as places where demons would haunt, such as in Is. 34:13-14. It was a place where the unclean animals gathered. The unclean animals, such as the screech owl, the jackal, the wild hairy goat, the pelican, the ostriches, and the arrow snake, all represent some sort of demonic spirit. The Greek word for 'waterless' is the word 'anudros.'[8] This is the same word also found in 2 Pet. 2:17, which refers to the unclean, deplorable state of false teachers who were compared to clouds without water or 'waterless.'

2 Pet. 2:17   "These are waterless springs and mists driven by a storm. For them, the gloom of utter darkness has been reserved" ESV.

The New Living Translation says, "These people are as useless as dried-up springs or as mist blown away by the wind." There is a corresponding relationship between spiritual dryness and demonic habitation. The

---

[8]"Anudros," Strong's Concordance #504, https://biblehub.com/greek/504.htm

last thing anyone should want in life is to live in such a way that demons feel at home. This teaches us just how important it is for us to maintain a healthy relationship with the things that keep us well watered – prayer, worship, time spent with the Lord and in His word, and even fellowship with other believers to keep our spirits thriving and whole.. However, an even greater watering can take place internally. Jesus told the Samaritan woman at the well that if she had the well of living water, she would never thirst again!

John 7:38   "Whoever believes in me, as the Scripture has said, 'Out of his heart will flow rivers of living water.'"

John 4:14   "But whoever drinks the water I give him will never thirst. Indeed, the water I give him will become in him a fount of water springing up to eternal life."

Jesus was referring to the gift of the Holy Spirit, which He later made available to every believer. It has been promised that we could draw water with joy from the well of salvation. We can fill the dry, empty places in our souls so that demons no longer feel welcome and at home!

Each person has various places, or rooms, where the enemy can potentially hide, especially if the individual has given ungodly spirits legal grounds to take up residence through sinful actions. A demonic spirit may not be able to inhabit the holiest place – our heart – because that is where the Holy Spirit dwells. However, evil spirits can take up residence in any part of the body that is not sanctified to the Lord.

Rom. 6:16   "Don't you realize that you become the slave of whatever you choose to obey? You can be a slave to sin, which leads to death, or you can choose to obey God, which leads to righteous living"

1 Cor. 6:9,10   "Do you not know that the wicked will not inherit the kingdom of God? Do not be deceived: Neither the sexually immoral, nor idolaters, nor adulterers, nor men who submit to or perform homosexual acts, nor thieves, nor the greedy, nor drunkards, nor verbal abusers, nor swindlers, will inherit the kingdom of God."

Gal. 5:20-12   "The acts of the flesh are obvious: sexual immorality, impurity, and debauchery; idolatry and sorcery; hatred, discord, jealousy, and rage; rivalries, divisions, factions, and envy; drunkenness, carousing, and the like. I warn you, as I did before, that those who practice such things will not inherit the kingdom of God … ."

WISDOM TO DEFEAT THE ENEMY

If a person has committed sexual sins, for instance, and cannot get free from certain sinful behaviors, it could very well be due to the fact that a demon of lust or a perverse spirit has been given legal rights to that particular body part. "I have the right to do anything," you say — but not everything is beneficial.

"'I have the right to do anything,'"—but I will not be mastered by anything. You say, "Food for the stomach and the stomach for food, and God will destroy them both." The body is not meant for sexual immorality but for the Lord and the Lord for the body. By his power, God raised the Lord from the dead, and he will raise us also. Do you not know that your bodies are members of Christ himself? Shall I then take the members of Christ and unite them with a prostitute? Never!

'Do you not know that he who unites himself with a prostitute is one with her in the body? For it is said, "The two will become one flesh." But whoever is united with the Lord is one with him in Spirit. Flee from sexual immorality. All other sins a person commits are outside the body, but whoever sins sexually sins against their own body. Do you not know that your bodies are temples of the Holy Spirit, who is in you, whom you have received from God? You are not your own; you were bought at a price. Therefore, honor God with your bodies.' - 1 Cor. 6:12-20, NIV.

This scripture proves a point. A spirit of prostitution (or the spirit of adultery) can become one with the flesh. Lust can reside in the soul or even the eyes because the eye gate is where lust is conceived.

1 John 2:16   "For all that is in the world—the desires of the flesh, the desires of the eyes, and the pride of life—is not from the Father but from the world."

Luke 11:34-35   "The lamp of the body is the eye. Therefore, when your eye is good, your whole body also is full of light. But when your eye is bad, your body also is full of darkness. Therefore, take heed that the light which is in you is not darkness."

Luke 11:34-35 reminds us that we need to continually allow the word of God to illuminate our darkness and cleanse our hearts. If we do not, the windows of our soul may become darkened, giving the enemy a place to influence how we 'see.' What we see and how we see it determines whether or not we will act upon certain impulses. The government of God is among us because He has written His laws on our hearts, but we must submit them to the Lord and allow Holy Spirit to take His rightful place in our lives. We must yield to His authority through humility and repentance before we can resist the devil and expect him to leave.

If a person has used their hands, for instance, for dishonorable purposes and sin against themselves or others, they have yielded that particular part of their body to evil, not God. If a person has allowed their tongue to be used for gossip, strife, division, anger, vengeance, or slander, then they have yielded that body part to be used by the devil for his purposes. They have not brought their mouth under submission to God's authority. The hands, the sexual organs, and the mouth are all examples of how evil spirits can take up residence in various rooms of our house. The body has many rooms, but so does our soul.

Unhealed wounds, offenses, negative memories of traumatic events, bitter root judgments, internal vows, shame, agreements with negative words, twisted perceptions of God, feelings of abandonment or rejection, and lies in a person's belief system are all examples of various 'rooms' in the soul. These are places where the enemy can take up residence and create a stronghold in a person's belief system.

Alexander Pagani, in his book *The Secrets to Deliverance* writes, "Deliverance is not a power encounter, but a truth encounter! The more truth you understand, the freer you become and the more any areas (rooms) in your life where demons are hiding become exposed and resolved." [9] It is also important to understand that once demonic spirits have been identified, the individual has a responsibility (confession and repentance) and then there is the responsibility to command the spirit to leave. If it is not commanded out it will remain.

Our words can either give devils access to us or our words can help close the doors to the enemy. When deliverance is effective it results in people becoming free and healed. It is very important not to leave that space empty. Remember what was previously mentioned about the dry, waterless places. Invite the Holy Spirit to fill that place, to reveal light and truth. Speak blessing over that room in the soul. If it is a body part that has been delivered from an evil spirit and sanctified to the Lord, bless it. Speak what is pure, right and declare that it will no longer be used as an instrument of unrighteousness, but for God's intended purpose.

There is another way that demonic spirits can take up residence in body parts that causes sickness and disease. As in the case of inherited disease, there is physical weakness in the genes or DNA of a family towards certain health issues. Sometimes that is a result of an unbroken curse. I am not saying that every physical disease is spiritually rooted, however, I do believe that many times the spiritual roots are overlooked. If you examine the function of the affected body part and its purpose in the body sometimes you can figure out what type of questions to ask.

What toxic thoughts, beliefs or negative self-talk is the person dwelling on?

---

[9] Pagani, Alexander. The Secrets to Deliverance, Charisma House Publisher, pg.29.

What body parts are being affected by sickness, weakness or disease?

What is that body part's function, and is there a spiritual parallel where the body is manifesting a spiritual truth?

Andy Glover, in his book **Double Portion: Our Inheritance** writes, "There have been a number of times in my life when I have harbored unforgiveness in my heart in relation to different individuals. These people have then become prominent in my thinking and feelings, and have ultimately influenced my decision making. I can't get them off my mind and when their names are brought up all the negative thoughts and emotions rise to the surface. My heart starts to suffer and I go through an emotional torture." "When your heart is connected to someone in unforgiveness, then it is not free to fully connect with your heavenly Father."[10]

Getting down to the root of emotional issues often reveals someone that needs to be forgiven. It can also reveal ungodly agreements the person has made about themselves. So much of what we carry with us on a daily basis is retained in painful memories and the trauma of past events. Those wounds become open doors to the enemy which grant spirits of darkness access to our heart and lives. These things take up residence in the very cells of our bodies, creating room for illness, disease, infirmity and a whole host of other physical, emotional and spiritual problems. We know this is true because certain emotions can trigger hormonal responses, and hormones trigger physical responses. The issues between what is going on in our soul are often connected to what's going on in our bodies. Sometimes the issue in our physical body points right back to a spiritual reality. God wants to heal us so deep it touches the very core of our being and regenerates healing from the inside out.

One example of a spiritually rooted health condition is auto-immune disorders. Auto immune disease can often be rooted in self-hatred, self-rejection, father issues, a sense of parental abandonment, and an orphan spirit. When the person rejects themselves, the body comes into agreement and the white blood cells begin to attack the body. That's not to say this is always the case, however. Dietary reactions to certain foods can make people ill, and there are other issues that can affect the physical body. Some people don't produce certain hormones, chemicals or enzymes for their bodies to function correctly, and it can lead to disease. Vaccinations also work to slowly destroy the immune system, through the introduction of heavy metals and other adjuvants. Regardless of the cause, however, we still serve a God that works miraculously to reverse physical situations to heal and restore our bodies.

---

[10] Glover, Andy: Double Portion, Our Inheritance, pg.60

The bones are another example of things that can contribute to spiritually rooted sickness and disease. The bones are used to create bone marrow. It's where our body produces red blood cells. So, if there is an issue with the blood or the bones, then we ought to examine what the scriptures tell us about the bones.

UNCONFESSED SIN REMOVES THE HEALTH: "There is no soundness in my flesh because of thine anger; neither is there any rest in my bones because of my sin" The Holy Bible: Psalm 38:3.

UNCONFESSED SIN DRIES THE BONES: "When I kept silent, my bones waxed old through my roaring all the day long" The Holy Bible: Psalm 32:3.

SIN FILLS THE BONES: "His bones are full of the sin of his youth, which shall lie down with him in the dust" The Holy Bible: Job 20:11

SHAME CAN ROT THE BONES: "A virtuous woman is a crown to her husband: but she that maketh ashamed is as rottenness in his bones" The Holy Bible: Proverbs 12:4.

CURSING MAKES THE BONES UNSOUND: "As he clothed himself with cursing like as with his garment, so let it come into his bowels like water, and like oil into his bones" The Holy Bible: Psalm 109:18.

FEAR & ROTTENNESS CAN CAUSE AN ENEMY TO TAKE UP RESIDENCE IN THE BONES::

"When I heard, my belly trembled; my lips quivered at the voice: rottenness entered into my bones, and I trembled in myself, that I might rest in the day of trouble: when he cometh up unto the people, he will invade them with his troops" The Holy Bible:: Habakkuk 3:16.

A BROKEN SPIRIT DRIES THE BONES: "A merry heart doeth good like a medicine: but a broken spirit drieth the bones" The Holy Bible: Proverbs 17:22.

GRIEF FROM INIQUITY CAUSES THE BONES TO BE CONSUMED: "For my life is spent with grief, and my years with sighing: my strength faileth because of mine iniquity, and my bones are consumed" The Holy Bible: Psalm 31:10.

BUT, THE FEAR OF THE LORD PRODUCES HEALTH IN THE BONE MARROW: "Be not wise in thine own eyes: fear the LORD, and depart from evil. It shall be health to thy navel, and marrow to thy bones" The Holy Bible: Proverbs 3:7-8.

A GOOD REPORT MAKES THE BONES FAT: (PRODUCES HEALTHY RED BLOOD CELLS IN

BONE MARROW: "The light of the eyes rejoiceth the heart: and a good report maketh the bones fat" The Holy Bible: Proverbs 15:30.

A CLEAR CONSCIENCE REJOICES THE BONES: "Behold, thou desirest truth in the inward parts: and in the hidden part thou shalt make me to know wisdom. Purge me with hyssop, and I shall be clean: wash me, and I shall be whiter than snow.   Make me to hear joy and gladness; that the bones which thou hast broken may rejoice" The Holy Bible: Psalm 51:6-8.

PLEASANT WORDS RESTORES BONE MARROW: "Pleasant words are as a honeycomb, sweet to the soul, and health to the bones" The Holy Bible: Proverbs 16:24.

DELIVERANCE REJOICES THE BONES: "All my bones shall say, LORD, who is like unto thee, which deliverest the poor from him that is too strong for him, yea, the poor and the needy from him that spoileth him?" The Holy Bible: Psalm 35:10.

ENVY ROTS THE BONES. "A sound heart is the life of the flesh but envy is rottenness to the bones" The Holy Bible: Prov. 14:30.

We know that the life is in the blood; therefore, if the blood is being attacked, or the bones that are responsible for creating the marrow and blood cells are sick and diseased, then we need to explore the possibility of a curse that needs to be broken. The previous scriptures are not an exhaustive list but they do offer proof that the bones are another 'room' where spirits of infirmity can hide. It becomes very important to consider family history because there could be contributing factors to disease or issues that originate in the bones.

As with auto-immune issues, we realize that when the part of the body that is supposed to contribute to the body's health and defense begins to shut down, there can be a spiritually rooted issue that is contributing to the problem. Perhaps not always, but enough that one definitely does not want to disregard the possibility. The poetic language in scripture is not just figurative, it contains a spiritual truth. Many of the things mentioned in the scriptures are actually demonic spirits. Shame, cursing, fear, envy, pride (that causes silence, or a lack of repentance) are demonic spirits. The spirit of infirmity is another one. These spirits can occupy rooms of our spiritual house.

Psalm 91 gives us a blessing and a promise to those that seek their refuge in the Lord Jesus Christ. In verse 10, the word 'plague' is from the Hebrew word 'nega.' It is translated as: 1) a stroke or a blow, figuratively or inflicted {inflicted by man on man}; 2) also a second meaning, {stroke, metaphor, especially of a disease, regarded as sent by a divine chastisement}; 3) plague or a mark {regarded as the heavy touch or stroke of a disease}. The Strong's Concordance translates it like this: affliction, assault, infection, mark {regarded as the heavy touch or stroke of a disease, such as leprosy}, plague, plagues, stripes, stroke, strokes, wounds.[11]

God has given us an amazing promise. If we make the Lord our dwelling place, evil shall not befall us and neither shall any plague come near us. Regardless of where the wound originated, God has made a provision to be free and healed from it!

Do you remember the promise of Passover? The Israelites were spared from the death of the firstborn because of the blood of the lamb on the doorposts. They were spared from the plague of death because of the blood - just as you are also now spared from the lasting effects of being plagued by wounds inflicted from the enemy. Jesus's blood has healing power to restore those areas of your mind, body, and soul. Whatever you are struggling with, whatever the enemy has aimed against you - place it into one of the stripes Jesus took for you. Matthew 8:17 tells us that "He himself took our infirmities and bore our sicknesses."

Therefore, we can declare "By His stripes we are healed." Agreeing with God's word is key; we must believe that God can, He wants to, and has already made the provision for our healing. Faith is active participation with God so that we can receive what we are believing to receive! God has made provision for every need you have. I guarantee you there is a specific promise for you in His word. You just need to ask Him what it is and begin to declare the blood of Jesus has made it possible.

When we receive Jesus as our Lord and Savior, something supernatural happens. We become a new creation. The blood of Jesus washes away our sin, and he gives us a new heart. He changes us from the inside out, and His Spirit comes to live inside of us. That is why Romans 6:11 reminds us to count ourselves dead to sin but alive to God as we are "in" Christ Jesus. He has made it possible to have unbroken fellowship with Him. As newborn babes in the faith, God takes us out of the realm of darkness, lifts us up, and brings us home. Romans 8:15 declares this beautiful truth, that we have been adopted into the family of God!

No longer feeling like an orphan, we experience the reality of being loved, valued, and accepted by our Father. The adoption papers have been signed. It's official! Galatians 3:26 tell us that *"in Christ Jesus"* we are all sons of God through faith. The law of the Spirit of Life which is *in Christ Jesus* frees us from the law of sin and death. He tenderly cares for us and hides us inside Himself. He brings us into His house where

---

[11] Strong's Concordance #5061, https://biblehub.com/hebrew/5061.htm, accessed Aug. 23, 2018

He can watch over us and keep us safe. God the Father puts us in the safest place possible – *in Christ*. But He doesn't stop there. He puts the Spirit of Christ *in us*.

1 Cor. 3:16   "Do you not know that you are a temple (a house) and that the Spirit of God dwells in you?"

The treasure of the Holy Spirit has been entrusted to us. God has put His Spirit within us, according to Ezek. 36:27 and 1 Cor. 3:16. So, the love of the Father compels Him to protect us. He puts Christ inside of us, He puts us in Christ, and He wraps us up in love like swaddling a baby. He made absolutely sure nothing could separate us from His love, and He makes our heart His home. We are safe in Christ, no matter what may be going on around us. We are the spiritual house that Jesus came to restore.

Have you ever had a nightmare? Do you remember how much better you felt when someone turned on the lights and showed you everything was ok and you were safe? In the same way, doesn't it make sense to let Him into every room in our house? Take the flashlight and peer into every dark corner to make sure nothing scary is trying to hide there? Trust in the Lord with all your heart. He will give you victory as you allow Him access to every part of your heart and life!

CHAPTER EIGHT
COURTS OF HEAVEN

In Luke 18:1-8 there is a story about a woman who continued to approach an unjust judge in her city to petition him for justice. Jesus gave a parable about this woman which I will include below:

'Then He spoke a parable to them, that men always ought to pray and not lose heart, saying: "There was in a certain city a judge who did not fear God nor regard man. Now there was a widow in that city; and she came to him, saying, 'Get justice for me from my adversary.' And he would not for a while; but afterward he said within himself, 'Though I do not fear God nor regard man, yet because this widow troubles me I will avenge her, lest by her continual coming she weary me.'"

Then the Lord said, "Hear what the unjust judge said. And shall God not avenge His own elect who cry out day and night to Him, though He bears long with them? I tell you that He will avenge them speedily. Nevertheless, when the Son of Man comes, will He really find faith on the earth?"'

This example illustrates a court situation with God as our judge, as well as the need to persist in prayer and not give up until an answer comes. There are times when it seems as though our prayers are just stuck and we don't know why. It is not because God doesn't want to answer, but He is teaching us persistence and patience. There are times when God wants us to seek Him for a particular answer that comes by revelation. He knows the breakthrough isn't going to happen without prophetic insight or a word of knowledge. This is the whole essence behind this type of teaching. It teaches us to listen for spiritual keys that will unlock something in the spirit realm.

When we are faced with trials, temptations, frustrations, and difficulties, they can definitely take their toll on our emotions. However, we cannot approach God in our pride, anger, or self-righteousness. The only proper response when approaching the just Judge of all heaven and earth is humility. He resists the proud but gives grace to the humble. We have access to His throne at any time, and we can come boldly to the throne of grace to find help in the time of our need!

There are different levels of the heavenly realms. We know this is true because the Apostle Paul spoke about visiting the third heaven.

Ephesians 6:12 tells us, "For we do not wrestle against flesh and blood, but against principalities, against powers, against the rulers of the darkness of this age, against spiritual hosts of wickedness in the heavenly places."

Through this, we understand that even though Satan was cast down from the highest heavens (where God dwells), he still has access to different levels of the heavenly realms. One of the names for the enemy is also called the Prince of the Power of the Air. So, even though Satan cannot necessarily go before the throne of God anymore, it would appear that he still can enter the courtroom and act as an accuser. Rev. 12:10 says that the accuser of the brethren accuses us before God day and night. This means Satan is constantly looking for any opportunity to act as a prosecuting attorney. Depriving others of justice is exactly what Satan does. His whole purpose of bringing a lawsuit against us in the court of heaven is to deny us what is rightfully ours. The good news is that we overcome by the blood of the Lamb and the word of our testimony!

Rev. 12:11 "And they overcame him because of the blood of the Lamb and because of the word of their testimony, and they did not love their life even when faced with death." NASB

The word for testimony in Rev. 12:11 is 'maturia,' as found in the Strong's Concordance, #3141. It means "what one testifies, as in a legal sense, before a judge." It also means to bear witness or give testimony of what we know about Jesus Christ. Sometimes we cannot testify on our own behalf, but our Paraclete and helper, the Holy Spirit, can testify on our behalf because He is close enough to the situations concerning our lives that He has seen every detail.

If you search for principles of scripture, you will discover that many New Testament words actually have legal definitions. The devil has only one job description: to kill, steal and destroy. He is constantly on the prowl to see whom he may devour. 1 Peter 5:8 says, "Be sober, be vigilant; because your adversary, the devil, walks about like a roaring lion seeking whom he may devour."

The word adversary in the above scripture comes from the Greek word 'antidikos,' which means an opponent (in a lawsuit); especially, Satan (as the arch-enemy) -- adversary. Antidikos is a technical legal term used to refer to a prosecuting attorney in a courtroom, someone seeking official (formal, binding) damages.[12]

---

[12] Strong's Concordance, "antidikos," from Biblehub.com accessed Mar. 7, 2018, http://biblehub.com/greek/476.htm, HAYER'S GREEK LEXICON, Electronic Database. Copyright © 2002, 2003, 2006, 2011 by Biblesoft, Inc. All rights reserved. Used by permission. BibleSoft.com

Matthew 5:25-26 is another scripture that references the adversary. In this portion of scripture, Jesus is talking about anger, slander and offense. He tells us to forgive others lest the adversary deliver us over to the judge, so as to avoid the possibility of being thrown into jail.

"Therefore, if you bring your gift to the altar and there remember that your brother has something against you, leave your gift there before the altar and go your way – First be reconciled to your brother and then come and offer your gift. Agree with your adversary quickly, while you are on the way with him, lest your adversary deliver you to the judge, and the judge hand you over to the officer, and you be thrown into prison. Assuredly, I say to you, you will by no means get out of there till you have paid the last penny."

Luke 12:58 reiterates this principle. We have an adversary that is looking for legal grounds to inflict suffering and the right to withhold what is ours. Unforgiveness will definitely block our ability to have prayers answered. It will block finances, is a cause for deterioration in emotional health and well-being, and it is a spiritual root for infirmity, disease and death. People often overlook unforgiveness as a reason why they cannot seem to prosper, but it is a very common door the enemy uses to his advantage. People often try to close various doors to the enemy on other issues but neglect the condition of their heart towards other people. Satan sees it as an open door to remain in the person's life. Unforgiveness can cause things to come to halt until it is dealt with properly. A prosecuting attorney must know the law and Satan uses it to his advantage. When we sin, we become a target for demonic attack.

"When you go with your adversary to the magistrate, make every effort along the way to settle with him, lest he drag you to the judge, the judge deliver you to the officer, and the officer throw you into prison. I tell you, you shall not depart from there till you have paid the very last mite." Luke 12:58 Here we see evidence that heavenly courts do exist.

Is. 43:26   "Now help Me remember. Let's get this settled. State your case and prove to Me you are in the right" The Voice Translation.

Satan, of course, is the prosecutor. He is known as the accuser of the brethren in Rev. 12:10. While we must do our part to be diligent and walk in obedience to God, the good news is that when we sin, we have an advocate – an attorney – that will speak on our behalf.

1 John 2:1   "My dear children, I am writing this to you so that you do not sin. But if anyone does sin, we have an advocate who pleads our case before the Father. He is Jesus Christ, the one who is truly righteous."

There are spiritual concepts and images that are portrayed by certain scriptures, and there are many references in the word of God that create visual imagery for the reader. Jesus frequently spoke in parables to illustrate a point and He did so for a reason. He spoke in language that was familiar to those around him. Certain scriptures definitely reference things you would find in a courtroom.

Isaiah 33:22   "For the Lord is our judge, the Lord is our lawgiver, the Lord is our king."

Of course, there is another reference to a courtroom setting in Daniel chapter 7 where it states that the 'court was seated,' and the enemy was prevailing until the Ancient of Days came and rendered a judgment on behalf of the saints. This is another scripture that proves heavenly realities. In the spirit realm exist kings and kingdoms, thrones and councils, courts and courtrooms. The next scripture reference proves that Jesus is our advocate and attorney.

1 Timothy 2:5   "For there is one God and one mediator between God and man[kind], [and that is] Christ Jesus."

Rom. 8:16   "The Spirit himself testifies with our spirit that we are children of God."

Do you see a courtroom portrayed in scripture? If there was no courtroom, why would we need an attorney? Yet, God has provided one. While we must do our part to be diligent and walk in obedience to God, the good news is that when we sin, we have an advocate – an attorney – that will speak on our behalf.

1 John 2:1   "My dear children, I am writing this to you so that you do not sin. But if anyone does sin, we have an advocate who pleads our case before the Father. He is Jesus Christ, the one who is truly righteous."

The Holy Spirit is our witness. The word for advocate in this scripture is the Greek word 'parakletos,' which means a legal advocate who makes the right judgment because he is close enough to the situation to know what is going on. It is the New Testament term for attorney (lawyer); in other words, someone that gives testimony that stands up in a court of law. Parakletos also references a helper, an advocate, an intercessor, a consoler and comforter. It is the same word Jesus used to describe the Holy Spirit.

We already covered the issue of how generational curses and unconfessed sin can hinder prayers from being answered. We know that the enemy always examines us for places where we have made some agreement with him and unintentionally surrendered our dominion or authority. I used to think that Satan could only operate if we had given him legal grounds to do so, but the enemy is known as a thief, and thieves are law breakers. Satan was thrown out of heaven because he broke the rules and acted in rebellion to God. He has never changed, and the enemy is still a law breaker. That means that there will be times when he does something that is completely against the law, but it's our job to catch him doing something illegally, take the situation to the court room and ask the judge to grant us a legal judgment in our favor. That is why the scripture says,

Prov. 6:31   "But if he is caught, he must pay back seven times what he stole, even if he has to sell everything in his house."

Do you notice that the scripture says, "IF he is caught?" You have to catch him before you can make him repay! How are you going to catch a thief? Through revelatory knowledge! There are many great teachings on the courts of heaven by various teachers. Some people may not choose to believe this is a valid teaching because they claim they cannot find it in scripture. However, these teachings were given by revelation from the Holy Spirit, and revelation is a powerful teacher. If we were to discount other people's revelations, experiences and testimonies simply because we didn't find the exact words in the Bible, we would miss out on a lot of valuable information.

Robert Henderson is a prophetic minister who has teachings on this subject, and his teachings are also a direct result of revelation and an encounter with God. One of the things he pointed out is that we can approach God on three different dimensions. The first one is as our Father, the second is as a friend, but the third way to approach God is as a judge. Judges rule over judicial systems, and we know that our God is a God of justice. Henderson makes a lot of great points, but allow me to sum up a testimony he shared in a meeting at Catch the Fire Toronto.

Robert explained how his son had gone through a very difficult time in his life after getting a divorce. His son was terribly depressed for two years. Robert prayed and did everything he knew how to do, but there was no change. Then one day, after praying for two years, Robert went to pray again for his son, but that time he heard the Lord tell him, "Bring your son to my courtroom." He said that he wasn't sure what to do, but he began by repenting on his son's behalf. As he explained, he could do so as an intercessor because intercessors pray for others until they are able to do it for themselves. Then he began to repent for any mistakes he had made as a father. The Lord told Robert to repent for the negative words he had spoken about his son out of frustration.

He didn't speak them *to* his son, but he spoke of his frustration to his mother, and the Lord told him that the enemy had used those negative words as an assignment against the son. The Bible says the power of life and death reside in the words we speak. The enemy found legal grounds to carry out certain assignments because he found someone to agree with a negative report. The Lord told Robert to repent for speaking negative words about his son's future and to begin to declare that his son would fulfill his destiny. Then the Judge of Heaven issued a judgment against the enemy. As Henderson testified, a short time later his son remarkably turned a corner and came out of the depression that had been holding him captive.[13]

PROTOCOL TO ENTER THE COURTROOM

1. **Humility**. Scripture tells us that God resists the proud but gives grace to the humble (1 Peter 5:5,6).

2. **Thanksgiving and praise** (Psalm 100:4).

3. **Blood covenant**. We do not come before God claiming to have any righteousness of our own. We approach God on the basis of what Jesus's shed blood has afforded to us (Heb. 10:19; Rom. 5:2, Eph. 3:12).

4. **Confession & Repentance** (1 John 1:9).

When we bring our own sins or those of our ancestors before God, we also identify with them. We have inherited everything that's been a part of our past, whether or not we wanted it. Prayers of repentance take responsibility for sin that never had the blood of Jesus applied to it and asked God to remove the enemy's inroad into our lives. We confess what we know before we come into the courtroom so that God will hear our prayers.

Part of the reason I find this effective is that it causes a person to earnestly seek God for His intervention and to listen to what is being communicated in the spirit. The enemy's voice is always waiting, ready to launch a fiery dart when he sees an opportunity or presents some sort of accusation. The enemy loves to bombard people's minds with accusations, toxic shame, fear, and dread. He wants people to feel insecure, inferior, and intimidated because if they do, they spend all their time battling negative emotions rather than taking authority over the accuser's voice and getting the victory. When the enemy comes to remind a person of their past, it's not a reflection on the individual as much as it is an accusation against the cross of Christ. John 3:19-21 in The Message says this:

"This is the crisis we're in: God-light streamed into the world, but men and women everywhere ran to the darkness. They ran for the darkness because they were not interested in pleasing God. Everyone who practices doing evil, addicted to denial and illusion, hates God-light and won't come near it, fearing a painful

---

[13] "Introduction to the Courts of Heaven," Robert Henderson, July 29, 2016, https://www.youtube.com/watch?v=4Xk2UChVsB0

exposure. But anyone working and living in truth and reality welcomes God-light so that God-work can be seen for what it is."

The accuser always looks for the opportunity to shame us into silence. He wants the guilt, condemnation, fear of rejection, and shame to keep our stories locked up inside of us. Satan tries to make us think that we have more to fear from the judgments of others than taking a step of faith, but the moment we tell the truth, whatever we feel ashamed about becomes a part of our past. It's *behind* us, and we can begin to heal. When we hold our story in, that shame and fear are still a part of our present reality. There is nothing worse than an untold story. Our soul bears the grief and the desire for redemption. We long to be known as the best version of ourselves, but it means facing the things we despise about ourselves and our past failures and allowing God to transform our story into something new.

He has already written **Redemption** over our life stories. Every mistake and failure has been rewritten into something beautiful in our books of destiny, so we don't need to fear transparency. People want to know what made us vulnerable, and the only way to talk about it is to share not only the pain, but the lies the enemy told us and how he manipulated our emotions so we can help others avoid the same traps. If we allow pain and emotional torment to stay locked up inside of us, it can become debilitating and emotionally destructive.

Unresolved pain often leads to other self-destructive behaviors. It can also sabotage your future and destiny because you will never reach those God wants you to reach without being authentic and transparent. Do yourself a favor and find a way to tell your story honestly, but also reframe your negative thoughts into positive ones. This will help you feel more confident in sharing your testimony. Tell people what you learned from that difficult situation. Talk to others about how the Lord met you and set you free.

Your testimony is how you overcome, and it gives others hope! So, remember, when someone brings up your past, it is usually because there is something critical or offensive in them. Retaining judgments against others places those who are guilty of them under judgment themselves, according to Matthew 6:15 and 7:1. When a person carries a grudge against someone else, they are the one that stands guilty before God, because they fail to believe in the power of Jesus's blood to redeem that person from sin.

Therefore, the Father must judge them according to His word. Perhaps someone else feels you are not truly forgiven until you jump through their hoops or pay some form of penance that makes them feel better. Perhaps they are trying to avoid conviction concerning other matters in their life. Many times, it is because they fail to recognize their own need for God's mercy or forgiveness.

On the other hand, sometimes we simply need to believe God's word and take it by faith that we truly are forgiven, then move forward. We have just as much a responsibility to take authority over the voice of the enemy when it attempts to work through a spirit of guilt, condemnation, discouragement, and unbelief toward the promises of God. If you have made an agreement with the accuser, then you must renounce that agreement and cover it in the blood of Jesus, asking that your repentance and the blood of Jesus void the agreement out.

When the enemy comes to remind you of your past – however he chooses to do it – enlist this visual aid as a form of help: See yourself walking into a courtroom. On one side, you are sitting behind a desk with your attorney. Who is your attorney? Jesus, of course!

He is standing right beside you. On the other side of the room, there are all your accusers. It could be things that others have said about you. You may even see yourself standing with them, agreeing with words others have said about you or negative words you have spoken about yourself.

The Judge has been seated. The Court is now in session.

(Say each name and what each person lists as charges against you. Or, you can ask God to make the enemy list the charges brought against you because he has found some legal grounds.")

If the situation is different and you feel it is the enemy withstanding your prayers for some unknown reason, then you can approach it this way:

"Your Honor, I ask that the adversary and my accuser be brought before the court, and list the formal charges against me. I would like You to make the adversary, Satan, acknowledge the legal grounds that have allowed him to withstand my prayers. What are the charges, your Honor?"

(Listen and pay attention to what you are shown. You may hear a voice in your spirit or be shown a memory of something you did. You could also see an image or hear certain words. What is God showing you?)

Out loud, say, "Your honor, these are my accusers. They are accusing me of _____ ".

THIS NEXT PART IS VERY IMPORTANT because you are forcing the enemy to reveal your blind spot. Acknowledge any area of sin or wrongdoing (for yourself, and just in case, include your ancestors), asking forgiveness and placing the blood of Jesus on each thing that is revealed. Then, ask again: "Your Honor, are there any other charges?" Go through the process again until there are no more charges. Each time apply the blood of Jesus, thanking God for Jesus's sacrifice that atones for your sin.

You: "I would like to call the Holy Spirit as my witness, your Honor. He knows everything about this case and can tell you what He knows."

Now, envision your attorney and ask Him to speak to the court on your behalf. If you could see and hear everything going on, it would sound something like this:

Jesus: "Excuse me, Your Honor, but I shed My blood for (insert your name). I became a sin for my client. Everything that the accusers list as charges against my client, I became for (insert your name.) when I took their sin upon the cross."

Jesus: "I became a bad parent. I took on the role of the rebellious, disrespectful child. I became an alcoholic, a gambler, a pedophile, a thief, an adulterer, a rapist, a drug dealer, or a murderer.

I became a failure. I became a source of pain to others. I became every one of their weaknesses, failures, and sins.

I became the curse on behalf of those for which I died. I was called every foul, shameful name people could muster up.

I was accused of every sordid, wicked thing that people did in secret. I became despised, rejected, and an outcast – for them.

I willingly took it all upon myself, and every sin and sick, the evil deed was nailed to my body as I was nailed to the cross.

I paid the price for them with My life and My blood. The Adversary cannot prosecute for a sin that has already been paid in full. The debt must be cleared from the records. I insist that You must acquit my client!"

Judge: "Granted. Defendant is NOT GUILTY."

I love what Jesus said in John 3:16-18. This is from the Message Translation:

"This is how much God loved the world: He gave His son, His one and only Son. And this is why: so that no one need be destroyed; by believing in Him, anyone can have a whole and lasting life. God didn't go to all the trouble of sending His Son merely to point an accusing finger, telling the world how bad it was.

He came to help, to put the world right again."

You're almost done, but there is something else that needs to be dealt with. You came to court to petition the court for something. Now is the time to ask for what you need.

You: "Your Honor, if I may, I would like to request something of the court. The law states in Proverbs 6:31 that if the thief is caught, he must repay with no less than a 7-fold return and also have to give up all the substance of his house. I ask for retroactive compensation for all the years of loss, according to Joel 2:25,26. I ask for full repayment as You did for the Shunamite woman in 2 Kings 8:7. I want everything that is mine, Your Honor! I want it all back! Jesus paid the price so that I could recover it all. I ask for relief from the Adversary, an eviction notice against him, and a restraining order as well. I ask that in the name of Jesus Christ, the Adversary and enemy would be bound and rendered completely immobilized, forbidden from taking action against me. I ask this in Jesus's name, amen."

(If there is something more specific you seek, speak exactly what you want done).

Finally, thank the Judge and the court for hearing your case and granting what has been requested. Prayers that serve to remove the legal grounds from the enemy can shift things in our lives and the lives of our entire family. These are strategic prayers that unlock destiny, restoration, finances, and much more.

This is the prayer that Ms. Elizabeth Nixon wrote and recited on Doug Addison's blog post How to Reclaim What's Yours in the Courts of Heaven.[14] I wrote about her teaching in one of my previous books called **Restoring the Glory**. This is an excellent prayer!

Elizabeth Nixon, "… If you think about the part of the territory that we're looking to get full ownership and occupation back over, it's our mental, emotional, physical, and spiritual selves. This is going to bring that quietness that you need. I am going to bring it in the Hebrews 12:23 heavenly court, where it says the Court of God is where God is Judge over all things. I am bringing it in the subdivision—the Romans 5:9 blood court, the Court of Redemption — where it says that you have been made right in God's sight by the blood of Christ, and He will certainly save us." Ms. Nixon's prayer is called "Petition to Quiet Title,' and it's a legal term used to reclaim real property from illegal squatters.

---

[14]Addison, Doug , How to Reclaim What's Yours in the Courts of Heaven, dated August 8, 2018. © Copyright 2018 Doug Addison and InLight Connection. All Rights Reserved . For more info on Elizabeth Nixon, please visit http://whitequillmedia.com/.

PETITION TO QUIET TITLE

"We bring a claim right now, Lord God, You who is judge over all things. And we bring it against the adversary, the accuser of the brethren.

Father, we say that there are personal, physical territories that he has been squatting on. There are emotional territories. We see this through trauma, depression, and anxiety. There are mental territories where we see oppression, torment, mental illness, and bipolar disorders. He is squatting on spiritual territories because of bloodline family issues, addiction, abuse, and genetic illness. He squats on finance territories for business and family finances, contracts, and even business opportunities. And he squats on geographical territories, whether that's a family ranch, a family home, or a city or a region that we are called to.

Lord God, we ask that the Adversary defendant be removed from our territories that he currently occupies, that he currently prevents us from having sole occupancy, possession, enjoyment, and ownership of. This adversary has entered our territories by illegally trespassing, and his presence is an illegal continued occupancy. He has no right to squat on our properties.

Father, we know that even though his trespass has nothing to do with our sins.

Father, there are areas where we are sin-free and clean, but he still comes in. Father, we choose to begin this petition prayer request with Acts 3:19.

Father, we repent of our sins and turn to God so that our sins might be wiped away. And Father, we come with a Psalm 51:17 contrite heart, that we know that You will not despise.

Father, we come according to James 4:7, which says we humble and yield ourselves before God. We resist the enemy so that he must flee. Father, we, in all humility before You, rebuke and resist the enemy. We put the adversary on notice that we intend now to occupy all of our territories and, therefore, the adversary must flee.

Regarding personal territories, Father, we know that we have been made in Your image. We know that the Earth and all of its people are yours. We belong to You, who have given us dominion over the Earth and ourselves. So, Father, the enemy, has no right to occupy those territories.

Father, we exercise authority over all power of the enemy. And we state in this case, again Luke 10:19, that we have liberty and the power of choice to influence and change these situations. We have a level of governmental rulership and judicial decision-making power, which we now operate in over all the power and authority of the enemy.

Lord God, Your Word says that we have been given this power and authority so that the enemy cannot violate us anymore. He cannot cause unjust consequences against us anymore. He has no power to perpetrate crimes against us. Father, I thank You that according to Galatians 3:13, 1 Corinthians 6:20, and 1 Peter 1:18, Your blood has paid the debt on all of our territories. Therefore, no debt exists on these territories, and the enemy cannot secure any ownership that trumps our authority. Moreover, according to Acts 4:12, there is no salvation in anyone other than the Name of Jesus. And 1 Timothy 2:5–6, there is one God and one Mediator between God and mankind, Christ, who gave Himself to redeem us.

Father, we claim and decree the Name of Jesus and His redemption over all of our territories. And we petition this Court for an order that requires the adversary to leave with no ability to secure legal ownership in any of our territories because he cannot pay the debt, and the debt has already been paid.

Lord God, this is the order that we request—that You enter a judgment ordering the heavenly Recorder of Deeds and Titles to confirm our territories as belonging to us, and that You will require the adversary to be removed from all territories that he presently occupies, and that You would grant any other relief that the Court deems is appropriate.

We acknowledge that we have three witnesses to this prayer petition today. In Romans 8:16, the Spirit Himself who testifies with our spirit; it is Revelation 1:5, Jesus Christ who is the faithful witness; and Revelation 3:15, the Amen, the faithful and true Witness, the Originator of God's creation.

Father God, You have the right to rule in our favor according to Colossians 1:16–17, where it says, for by God all things were created, all things that are in Heaven and in Earth, whether they are visible or invisible, whether thrones or dominions or principalities or powers, he created all things and for Him, and therefore they must serve Him. Father, we ask that You would cause our territories to be ours, our sole possession and that they will serve us according to Your purposes.

Father, I thank You now that You have granted a judgment in our favor. Father, that You render judgment in our favor and that You order the immediate and complete removal of the adversary from our territories, and that You order a Proverbs 6:31 sevenfold reparation and compensation for lost access and for damage to our territories in addition to late fees, penalties, and charges.

Father, I thank You that You are not only issuing that judgment, but also the angelic hosts — the Hebrews 1:4 angels — who are purposed to minister and to serve us, the heirs of salvation. And that You release now those angelic hosts to do for us what we cannot do for ourselves.

Father, cause Your hosts to be released to enforce the immediate physical and forceable removal of the adversary defendant from our territories and the immediate enforcement of sevenfold reparations.

Father, You purposed this from before the foundation of the world, and today You affirm it again in this Court. Father, we thank You that You have restored to us the fullness of our territories. You have restored our physical bodies. You have restored our emotions, mental abilities, and spiritual authority.

Father God, even the territorial lands, places, and people groups that you have called us to. You have restored them to us, and the enemy has been removed. Father, we worship Your Holy Name. We thank You, in Jesus' Name."

The following prayer is one I wrote to also specifically address issues pertaining to spiritual blocks to prayer concerning finances.

PRAYER TO UNLOCK FINANCES

Dear Heavenly Father,

I come before You into Your heavenly court, seeking relief from the enemy and the wicked oppressor, the thief who has robbed my family and me of the ability to prosper according to Your word.

I come to you, O God, as the heavenly Judge of all heaven and earth. I do not approach you on my own righteousness, for I have none; I approach you based on your goodness and mercy and because the Blood of Jesus has been shed for my sins.

I am a blood-bought child of God, and your word tells me I can find help in times of need.

The adversary and accuser have sought legal grounds to indict me and enforce a curse of poverty, financial lack, and an inability to prosper, thereby severely limiting my ability to influence others for the sake of the Kingdom of God.

Therefore, I ask you to hear my petition before the court.

On behalf of myself and others in my family line, I ask you to forgive our sins, transgressions, and iniquities.

Please forgive any misappropriation of finances in our history. Forgive us for poor stewardship, reckless spending, gambling, selfishness, and greed.

Forgive us for the times when we have had more than enough, and we did not spend it wisely, and the times when we acted miserly.

Forgive us for having the wrong motive and asking for things you could not bless because we asked for selfish intent.

Forgive us for the sin of hoarding, holding on to finances when you wanted us to be generous to others and to sow financial seeds.

Forgive us for having an attitude of entitlement, thinking that we deserved more when we had not proven we were trustworthy with finances.

Forgive us for having wrong expectations, expecting you to give us something when we had not wisely used what you had already given us.

Forgive us for neglecting to use our talents and abilities in the Kingdom of God and for failing to recognize our responsibility to invest the gifts, talents, and abilities so that they would bring an increase to your kingdom.

Forgive us for putting a monetary value on our service and for failing to serve others because we could not see the reward in it.

Forgive us for not serving you in joy and gladness, for the abundance of everything.

Forgive us for areas of unbelief and reluctance to release what's in our hand because we have doubted your goodness towards us.

Forgive us for serving and sowing from an attitude of stinginess and legalism rather than generosity and grace.

Forgive us for placing ourselves under Old Testament law instead of functioning in liberty and grace.

Forgive us for transgressing and being unable to fulfill the law.

Let us be released from the legalism attached to our mindset and giving.

Forgive us for having an evil eye toward others. Forgive us for allowing jealousy, envy, covetousness, idolatry, judgmentalism, and legalism to criticize others and pass negative judgments against them.

Forgive us for the pursuit of mammon, the sin of selfish ambition, and attempting to set up an idol of self-importance and self-sufficiency in the secret places of our hearts.

Forgive us for attempting to build our own kingdom rather than your Kingdom.

Forgive us for the sins of pride and self-righteousness, treating others with contempt and dishonor, character assassination, and uncovering the sins of others.

Forgive us for our unbelief and the inability to see you as good, gracious, and the source of all our blessing.

Forgive us for any areas where we have misled others and caused them to wander off the road of righteousness.

Forgive us for illegally and unlawfully attempting to seize what belonged to another person.

Forgive us for taking unlawful advantage of others.

Forgive us for taking a bribe, being a party to injustice, and robbing others of justice.

Forgive us for iniquity in our bloodline and anyone who made a covenant with demonic powers.

Forgive us for making a covenant with spirits of poverty, death, and hell, whereby we made lies our refuge.

Knowingly or unknowingly, we made a covenant with the wrong entities believing that those things could protect us, provide for us, and we placed our trust in the wrong gods.

Forgive us for selling ourselves into bondage either through sin or ungodly peace treaties, covenants, and contracts that have forced us into slavery, bondage, and service to others.

Forgive us for any advantages gained through immorality, bribes, trading services, and ungodly agreements and covenants.

I give back any advantages I may have received through demonic contracts and covenants.

I ask you, LORD, to restore the blessings you have for me.

Forgive us for any sacrifices and shedding of blood that was offered through the sins of murder, abortion, character assassination, slander, gossip, and evil speaking.

Father, you are the just Judge in the courts of heaven.

I ask my advocate and attorney, the Lord Jesus Christ, to intercede for me and speak on my behalf.

I also ask that Holy Spirit be called to give testimony and bear witness on my behalf, that I stand before you now forgiven and cleansed of all unrighteousness, according to 1 John 1:9.

I ask the court to revoke the legal grounds that the enemy has used to indict me and enforce a curse.

I petition the court to pass a favorable judgment on my behalf that annuls every demonic contract and old covenant.

I petition the court for angelic assistance to tear down every evil altar with my family name on it.

Let it be torn down now and our family name removed, in Jesus' Name.

I petition the court on behalf of any innocent blood shed; let the sacrifice be silenced, and all demonic portals are closed.

I ask that the blood of Jesus be applied to all altars, demonic thrones, and portals and seal them shut in Jesus' Name.

Finally, your honor, I petition the court for restoration and restitution to come forth immediately out of the enemy's storehouse.

According to your law in Proverbs 6:31 the thief, when caught, must repay at no less than a 7-fold return and have to give up the substance of his house.

Also, your honor, I ask that I be granted speedy recompense, retroactive compensation for the years the enemy has stolen from me, according to 2 Kings 8:3-6, Joel 2:23-27 and Luke 18:1-8.

Let the wealth once in my generational line be restored, and let it come into my hands now.

I ask you to bless us with creative ideas to create wealth and prophetic insight to know how to move with wisdom in economic shifts.

Father, I ask you to forgive my wrong mindsets and unbelief toward you.

Help me to overcome limited mindsets connected to a spirit of poverty.

I renounce all false gods, idols, and wrong beliefs that limit your ability to bless me. Help me to be financially free, a generous and joyful giver, a person you can trust with increase and prosperity, and to have the wealth that grants me influence for the sake of advancing the Kingdom of God. In Jesus's name, amen.

CHAPTER NINE
HEALING OF THE MEMORIES

Healing of the memories involves a process known as Theophostic Ministry. As with any other ministry or those that teach doctrine, we must exercise discernment to know whether or not they are abiding by the truth of God's word and being led by the Holy Spirit. We are counseled by scripture to 'test the spirits' according to 1 John 4:1. I have found this type of ministry quite effective because it is led by God's Spirit. The role of the ministry leader is simply to help the person being counseled ask the right questions and facilitate a conversation with the Holy Spirit. No other spirit is allowed to speak or minister to the person outside of Jesus, the Father, or the Holy Spirit.

Theophostic is a word derived from 'theos' (God) and 'phos' meaning (light). Theophostic Prayer Ministry was founded by Ed Smith in 1996. Smith teaches that all people are emotionally wounded and need inner healing. He teaches that a lie-based belief system is the core issue behind emotional pain, torment, and sin. The Holy Spirit is invited to meet with the individual and bring to mind old memories, situations, or traumatic events to shed light on the situation, helping the individual to identify the lies they may have believed about themselves, God, or a particular event in their life. In this way, the Holy Spirit is a revealer of truth, a comforter, and a bridge to connect the person to Jesus. The person is invited to revisit old issues so that they can see where Jesus was at the time the event occurred and receive a new perspective.

In our lifetime, we will experience pain, loss, suffering, rejection, and many things that God will use to make us more like Christ. Even Jesus suffered tremendously; however, God did not leave Jesus broken, rejected, and in emotional pain. Holy Spirit raised Jesus from the dead and gave him complete healing, victory, and dominion over all the power of the enemy. Then Jesus transferred His delegated authority to all born-again believers. God has promised to work all things together for our good, to those that love God and are called according to His purpose, (ref. Rom. 8:28).

God's promise to us in Is. 53:5 is that 'by His stripes, we were healed.' Jesus bought our healing. He doesn't expect us to live wounded or tormented by some demonic spirit. Where would be the victory in that? No, He gave us all authority over the works of the evil one, according to Luke 10:19.

In Mark 7:27, a woman approached Jesus, asking Him to heal her daughter. Her daughter was lying at home, suffering from demonic torment. Jesus's response at first was somewhat shocking; he told her she didn't have a right to ask for healing because she wasn't Jewish. This woman had no rights, but she continued to press Jesus anyway, and He relented. The woman went home to find her daughter healed. God's mercy and compassion are to show a willingness to heal, even to those that don't yet know Him in a personal relationship. It is the kindness of God that leads men to repentance.

Matt. 8:16-17 "When evening had come, they brought to Him many who were demon-possessed. And He cast out the spirits with a word, and healed all who were sick, that it might be fulfilled, which was spoken by Isaiah the prophet, saying: "He Himself took our infirmities and bore our sicknesses.""

It is clear that Jesus took the punishment for our sins and sickness upon Himself so that we could be healed. It's our right and privilege as children of God. So, right there, you know that God doesn't contradict His word. It's His will to heal and get His children out of pain. It's His word implanted in us, taken root in us, that heals us. Yes, God allows physical or emotional pain at times to provoke us to obey and to partake in the fellowship of Christ's sufferings. But, let us remember that Jesus died for our victory, health, restoration, and freedom.

Let's return to the heart of Theophostic ministry, and that is to invite Holy Spirit to uproot and reveal the lies in people's belief systems. It's not so much the past events that haunt us as it is the belief that we hold on to regarding those events. People may believe various lies, such as the thought that God abandoned them in a moment of fear, abuse, pain, or trauma. We know the truth of scripture teaches us that Jesus promises He will never leave us or forsake us according to Hebrews 13:5. However, sometimes a person needs to revisit a memory to break the power of the lie that they were left alone and defenseless in a difficult moment. When they 'see Jesus' in their situation with them, it dispels the lie so that the Spirit of Truth can reconcile the individual to the Lord. This process is quite gentle and effective. It allows the Holy Spirit to minister to the person, releasing the truth that will free them (ref. John 8:31,32).

2 Cor. 10:4-5 "For the weapons of our warfare are not carnal but mighty in God for pulling down strongholds, casting down arguments and every high thing that exalts itself against the knowledge of God, bringing every thought into captivity to the obedience of Christ ..."

There is a responsibility to the individual receiving counseling that once the lie has been revealed, they need to renounce it, ask forgiveness for believing it, and then break the agreement with the lie. The person can then ask for forgiveness (acknowledging their sin of unbelief), where the blood of Jesus then cleanses them of all unrighteousness according to 1 John 1:9.

There are many other lies that people believe can lead to strongholds in their belief system. Some examples might be a child that somehow believes they are responsible for their parents' divorce or a child that believes they are 'dirty or unclean' because of being molested. When hidden, underlying issues are exposed by the Spirit of Truth; it helps the person let go of internalized thoughts and feelings that lead to self-rejection, shame, guilt, and other negative emotions. When they realize they were not responsible for a negative situation, they can stop bearing the false burden of responsibility for another person's actions. Or, (depending on the type of situation involved) if there was some sort of responsibility on the part of the individual, they can then reconcile their assessment of the situation against the truth that is revealed by the Holy Spirit.

The basis of this type of ministry is to expose the lies that bind people to a false belief system in some area of their thought life. Recovery doesn't have to be a long, drawn-out process; it can occur in a moment when the Holy Spirit reveals the truth. It is beneficial to have someone else join you in a ministry session to help pray and also take notes.

Conducting a ministry session looks something like this:

Invite the person to sit down and make themselves comfortable. Begin by telling them what to expect. "We are going to invite Holy Spirit to speak to you and shed some light on a memory or event that is still causing you emotional pain and discomfort. After you pray, I want you to pay attention to your next thoughts. You may see a picture of something in your mind or think of some situation you had forgotten about. Are you ready to begin?"

After the person assures you they are willing to proceed, have them pray:

Holy Spirit,

I invite you to show me a memory or past event that you know needs healing. I give You permission to bring it out of my subconscious and into the light. I give you permission to unblock any repressed memories. I ask You to uproot any hidden lies in my belief system that the enemy is using to hold me in captivity. I know that You only desire what is good for me, and I can trust You. In the name and authority of the Lord Jesus Christ, I bind all evil spirits from trying to speak or influence this ministry session. I bind all lying spirits from feeding me deceptive information. Holy Spirit, what is it You want to heal today? Please, show me the truth that will make me free. In Jesus's name, amen.

Have the person sit quietly and listen for Holy Spirit to speak. Wait for them to reveal what they sense is a communication from the Holy Spirit.

The individual will probably begin to share something from their past. They may also experience painful emotions from that situation. Ask them what they felt at that moment. Then begin a series of questions and allow the Holy Spirit to show them His response.

What emotions are you aware of right now as you remember that situation/event?

(Write down what the person says. It may be rejection, shame, fear, fear of death, unlovable, etc.)

Pray: "Holy Spirit, what would you like to give me in place of (rejection, shame, fear, …)?"

Ask the person to inquire again of the Holy Spirit. "Holy Spirit, is there a lie I believed because of this particular situation? If so, what was it?"

Answer: "I believed I was _____." (Write it down)

Pray: "Holy Spirit, what is the truth?" (Write it down)

Pray: "Holy Spirit, where was Jesus when all this was happening to me?" (Write it down)

Pray: "Lord Jesus, what do You want me to know?" (Write it down)

Pray: "Lord Jesus, how do you see me?"

It is important to make sure that what the person believes they heard in prayer actually lines us with scripture. God is not going to violate His word. It is God's word implanted in us that is able to save us according to James 1:21. The word of truth sanctifies us according to John 17:17.

When the ministry leader is confident in what the individual heard, then that information can be used to take what was written down and use it to form a new prayer. Have the person recite the truth that they learned in the ministry session back to God. **(See sample prayer below)**

Father God,

I thank you that I am not rejected, but I am accepted in the Beloved according to Eph. 1:6,7. I repent for believing the lie that I was abandoned as a child when this situation happened. Your word affirms that You never left me, Jesus, according to Heb. 13:5. Even though I was unaware of Your presence, You were with me and have always watched over me. Thank You, Holy Spirit, for showing me that Jesus was with me, protecting me from something worse.

Thank you for showing me the truth. I am loved. Your word in Romans 5:8 reminds me of this fact. I am important because Jesus died for me. I am not unlovable. My Father has loved me since before the foundations of the world were created. Jesus assigned value to my life when He died in my place on the cross. I am not an orphan; I am a born-again child of God.

I renounce every lie and agreement with the kingdom of darkness. I renounce Satan as a false father, a liar, and a thief. I repent, Father, for making any agreements with demonic spirits that have given them legal grounds to be in my life.

I forgive (Parents, siblings, and other adults that caused pain or wounding, etc.) for creating an unsafe environment. I forgive them for betraying my trust and opening the door to the enemy.

I renounce any ungodly vows made in moments of emotional pain, fear, and trauma. I remove the walls that I put up between myself and others and between myself and You, God. Forgive me for keeping you at a distance. I give You permission to remove any other hindrances to my spiritual growth and intimacy. I thank you that in place of pain and trauma, You provide me with healing and wholeness, peace, and a restored sense of confidence that I am not inferior, insecure, or unlovable.

I recover all repressed memories. I rescue and recover everything the enemy took from me. I take back my self-esteem and identity as it is 'in Christ.' I reject everything concerning my old identity, and I break the power of condemnation in Jesus's name.

I let go of the disappointment and feelings of loss from the emotional bonding and nurturing I never received as a child. Heavenly Father, please give me something good and godly to replace that which I never received from my parents and family. Implant your love and assurance into my heart.

Let the blood of Jesus void all previous contracts and covenants. I forbid, in the name and authority of the Lord Jesus Christ, the curse from repeating itself. In Jesus's name, amen.

Each ministry session may uncover something new. Inner healing can be accomplished quickly and permanently through healing the memories. Once the lies are removed, the enemy can no longer use that as a weapon of emotional pain and torment against the individual. His perfect love casts out the fear that once ruled over the soul.

Forgiveness of ourselves and others is one of the greatest keys to moving forward. Retaining judgments, criticisms, resentment, and self-pity keeps us emotionally imprisoned. People that are emotionally stuck will often disassociate from painful experiences. Anything that shatters our sense of safety and security can cause us to feel very helpless and vulnerable. Families that experience a lack of necessary food, shelter, or resources can also suffer from emotional trauma because those issues create fear and worry and the feelings of being unsafe in a dangerous world. Neglect, deep betrayal, or abuse in any form also results in trauma. This creates stress and anxiety and may involve fear responses due to post-traumatic stress, where certain sounds, smells, or memories trigger anxious thoughts. It can even create phobias and chronic pain. Emotions create physiological responses, which cause our bodies to get stuck in 'fight or flight mode.'

When a person has trauma, their brain operates differently than a normal brain. The fear center in the brain is always on high alert, and it assesses everything to determine whether a threat is present. Emotional trauma can cause a person to feel scattered in their thoughts or lose certain memories altogether. It may be difficult to concentrate and stay focused. The mind tends to wander. Trauma creates fear, and fear is a lack of peace and safety. Our minds and responses are trained to help us feel safe. Responses include fleeing the difficult situation, shutting down, or perhaps feeling defensive, irritated, or a need to self soothe/self medicate. Our minds tend to gravitate towards avoidance where emotional trauma has occurred. Our soul becomes fragmented from our core because we have not truly understood who we were created to be, which is directly connected to our identity in Christ.

There are parts of our identity that may still need to be integrated into who we are at the core of our being. We must choose to be brave and face uncomfortable emotions and difficult realities that didn't measure up to the stories we told ourselves. We must stop making excuses for our own failures as well as the failures of others and allow ourselves to unearth the grief, heartbreak, loss, and disappointment. Learning how to surrender the betrayal and failures of meaningful relationships, the codes of conduct we learned as children, and permit ourselves to experience all the suppressed emotions, fears, and lies we believed, is what tears down the walls of fear, shame, guilt, and self-preservation that block our ability to grow and heal. Until we let go of all of it and decide we want no benefit from those things, we cannot get free or move forward.

We learn to replace certain behaviors, such as people pleasing, with healthy boundaries and realize the trap of perfectionism is driven by a deep need for validation and security. All our deficits stem from unmet needs that become drivers of our behavior. It is a yearning for some valid need to be met, so it is important to realize that our deepest needs are not bad desires, but equally important to understand that how we attempt to meet those needs can be misguided and result in disappointment if we look outside of the love and provision of God. Not everything we desire is what God wants for us. As we keep our hearts fixed on God, all our needs are met through the love and tender care of the One who gave His life for us. We learn to silence our inner critic, choose compassion towards ourselves and others, and set ourselves on a path for healing.

Part of acceptance is understanding that we are not bad simply because we have had to live through undesirable or negative experiences. Denial of painful truths only keeps us fragile, confused, and without answers to the need for healing. It took me many, many years to understand that for most of my life, I never felt a sense of safety or security. I lived in a constant state of stress and found it extremely difficult to be at rest. This is because my emotions got stuck, and I couldn't calm down or feel at peace.

For as long as I can remember, my childhood was dysfunctional, unstable, and full of fear. I struggled with deep loneliness, insecurity in my environment, and the fear of abandonment. After my mother remarried during my early teen years, the home environment was extremely uncomfortable, and I became inexplicably and repeatedly sick without any known reason. My stepfather was a narcissist and a liar, and made life difficult at home. I was deeply depressed and hated my life. I looked for a way of escape and ended up marrying a young man straight out of high school that was also a narcissist, a pathological liar, violent and abusive. Fear escalated into a terrorist in my life. Even after we divorced, this man stalked me for a couple of years. My car was vandalized repeatedly, he drained my finances, and broke into two different apartments. He threatened to take my child to another state in an effort to force me to return to him. I was worn-out, just trying to survive.

It seemed like I continued to find myself in different situations where I continually had to deal with individuals with Narcissist Personality Disorder (NPD). Narcissists are famous for belittling, gaslighting, and other shame-based interactions that blame others and cause them to doubt themselves. People with NPD refuse to take responsibility for their own actions and are famous for flipping the narrative to make themselves seen as either innocent of wrongdoing or a victim. This is largely in part because they are so self-absorbed that they rarely, if ever, think that they have done anything wrong. Their behavior is often abusive towards others and can range from mild to extreme. The personality traits of a person with NPD undermine the sense of safety, security and identity in those they target. People with NPD are also extremely competitive. Underlying low self-esteem contributes to jealousy and criticism of others, and they often feel a need to make others feel small so that they continue to feel superior. Although they can be charming when it suits them, they are also very manipulative, and it's like dealing with a person with a split personality.

I was saved when I was in my early thirties, and I thought I would finally find a healthy environment where I could begin to heal. As it turned out, there were several in the church leadership that had NPD. The jealousy, competition, and mind games were very unsettling, and I started to think maybe I was going insane. I did not know why I kept running into people with the same sort of abusive personality. At the time, I did not understand narcissism or know how to identify it, but I certainly recognized the spirit at work because it was very familiar. This little church became the birthplace of the prophetic in my life because God opened up the seer realm. Suddenly, I could SEE the demons that were in those individuals, and it was like they were looking right through me.

I saw an evil, murderous spirit in them, and without anyone having to say a word, those spirits communicated that they wanted to kill me. As a person that was new to the church and new to understanding the spiritual realm, it was very unsettling! Again, the atmosphere was charged with fear and intimidation, but God kept me there to learn and grow. I realized later that the demons recognized the **Spirit of Christ** in me, and that is what they despised and feared. The demons that tried to destroy Christ still hated Him and wanted to destroy anyone that could recognize them! God gave me a greater understanding of how the demonic realm strategizes and carries out assignments to produce curses, emotional wounding, and brokenness, reproducing these cycles over and over again, from generation to generation.

Demons cooperate with one another to draw people into relationships where they can continue to batter and abuse them, hoping they will give up on their faith and become so defiled they are unfit for the Master's use. What I did not realize until much later was that God used those situations to train me in spiritual warfare. He was training me to be an overcomer and to expose the tactics of the enemy so that others could get free.

During all those painful years, I had no time to try to process the emotions of things that happened to me before another painful event occurred. The negative cycles of abuse and brokenness that created more rejection, insecurity, shame, and fear continued for many years. My life was marked by:

- Addictions and repeated overdoses.
- Suicidal tendencies.
- Repeated loss of employment.
- Rape.

- The fear of losing my daughter because I couldn't hold myself together.

- Verbal abuse and accusation. Physical abuse.

- Religious/Spiritual abuse.

My life was so severely broken I did not know how to manage the stress, and I didn't trust anyone. The enemy worked overtime to bury me under layer after layer of guilt and shame. All I wanted was to feel safe and protected, but it seemed like that was beyond my grasp for much of my life. All of it culminated in getting physically, emotionally, and relationally stuck in myriad ways. Thankfully, God did not leave me in that place but continued to work with me to bring me into health and restore my emotions. He is my stability, and He can be yours, too, if you trust Him.

Getting free from demonic oppression is just one part of releasing us into greater levels of inner freedom. Still, we must also work on dealing with unresolved emotional issues and understanding how our neural pathways may need time to heal. Hormones need to be re-balanced, and we also need to replace certain beliefs and behaviors with more positive ones. Stress and trauma take time to unravel, so be gentle with yourself and others.

Grief, shame, bondage and addictions, broken relationships, trauma, fear, bitterness, witchcraft, and other things can be rooted in generations past as something we are born into. Though we didn't ask for it, we must still take responsibility if we want to live emotionally healthy lives. It's an evil inheritance that we must learn to cut off so that we can begin to heal and help our families break the negative cycles that have had us bound. Healing is far more complex than getting free from demonic oppression. It also involves breaking down negative thinking patterns, renewing the mind with the word of God, changing behavior, and positioning ourselves in humility and obedience for a breakthrough.

CHARACTER ISSUES CAN PREVENT BREAKTHROUGH

Many people pick up some negative personality traits in life, but if we are seeking a breakthrough in our lives, it's an important point to bring up. There are some things that God won't bless, and there are things the rest of the world doesn't find appealing, either.

The things we go through shape who we become. Sometimes we don't even know who we really are without all the negative characteristics that have been a part of us. Our heavenly Father wants us to discover who He created us to be without all the defense mechanisms and unhealed emotional wounds, and that only comes through our surrender. Abrasive personalities rub people the wrong way and can be why some doors of opportunity remain closed. For example, someone that is selfish, coldhearted, critical, and insensitive towards how their words and actions affect others can be perceived as an individual that is cunning, calculated, petty, and may have hidden agendas.

Words reveal the spirit at work as well as the fruit in people's lives. If people carry an offense, they attempt to mask unresolved anger and resentment, but at some point, negative emotions will expose themselves. Bitterness is unfulfilled vengeance, and it is also the root of rebellion and witchcraft. A person with bitterness will find it very difficult to submit to authority. They *will* cause offense because a bitter root defiles many others. If someone's words are toxic, it will create hurt and offense in others because bitterness is a form of misery. These are undesirable personality traits that will undermine unity, teamwork, and a peaceful environment. Lying, blame-shifting, and other petty behaviors display a lack of integrity and indicate red flags that a person is likely to prove untrustworthy and may become a potential source of trouble.

These types of negative personality traits and others are undesirable and can block a person's ability to obtain their personal and professional goals, and these negative qualities will also block answers to prayer. The Lord is very patient with us and wants us to develop certain qualities of Christ-like behavior, but the good fruit in our lives comes from being healed. He doesn't want bad fruit in us to defile others, so He will wait as long as it takes for us to surrender to His healing process before He opens the doors He has for us.

When God looks for someone to promote, He looks for certain qualities, such as faith, obedience, dependability, loyalty, honesty, integrity, kindness toward others, and humility. It does not matter how much knowledge we may have. If we truly know God, we keep His commandments and reflect His moral character. What matters most to the Lord is whether we have learned how to love Him in the secret place, to live in the light of His truth, and show mercy and love to others.

Shame can only exist in the darkness and isolation of our souls, but truth and empathy unravel toxic shame and other negative emotions. Living in the light brings us into fellowship with God, where confession of sin and conversation with the Lord assures us we are not rejected. We are accepted. We are forgiven. This assurance allows us to accept and embrace the perfect love that casts out all fear. In His presence is fullness of joy, and fear cannot remain in the presence of God. That is why getting into a secret place with God is so important.

Peace has to be cultivated. It takes intentionality to learn new responses that will help us get into position so we can experience peace. Getting into the secret place automatically positions us for victory and our enemies for failure. The secret place of intimacy with God is where He shares wisdom and strategies. When the love of God surrounds us, we feel secure and safe. A sense of safety must be *experienced,* and this is where God begins to transform our pain into power. When the environment is right, we begin to heal.

The revelation of our Father's love causes darkness to disappear. We learn that we are not alone, and God has provided people who help set us free. Willpower alone cannot heal us, but even chronic pain, illnesses, and other physical maladies can be healed as the emotions are healed, and the individual focuses on self-empowerment. When vulnerability and transparency meet compassion and understanding, darkness loses its grip.

CONCLUSION
MAINTAINING YOUR HEALING

It takes effort to get free, to learn how to walk in the Spirit, and to maintain your healing. None of us are perfect, of course, but when we recognize an area of unbelief or sin, we immediately take authority over it in prayer and don't let it linger. Practice these things frequently and consistently to ensure that you don't lose your healing!

- Renounce any agreements made in the spirit realm so that you don't give the enemy his next assignment.

- Repent for any wrongdoing or grieving the Holy Spirit.

- If you have allowed sin in your life, do what is necessary to remove it completely. Use wisdom, and don't return to the sin that will take you back into captivity.

- Remember to ask for prayer when you feel weak or vulnerable.

- Stay accountable to others in your life, and remain humble. Let others speak into your life and invite them to pray with you.

- Refuse to stay angry. Stay rooted and grounded in love, forgiving any offenses quickly. Bless those that you might feel tempted to feel offended with so that the enemy cannot get a foothold in your life.

- If you have offended someone else, be quick to ask for forgiveness so that the enemy cannot bring an accusation against you in the court of heaven.

- Stay connected to the Lord in His Word through obedience and prayer.

- Practice being grateful frequently and abundantly. Tell the Lord all the things you are thankful for!

- Declare the word of God and His promises over your life consistently!

Made in the USA
Middletown, DE
28 February 2023

25764421R10084